THIS IS THE
WORD
OF THE
LORD

Revised/Expanded Edition

THIS IS THE WORD OF THE LORD

**Readings of the Liturgy Arranged in
Dialogue Form for Presentation
by Three Readers**

Arranged by
William J. Freburger

Ave Maria Press † Notre Dame, Indiana 46556

William J. Freburger is the editor of *Celebration: A Creative Worship Service.* He is the co-author (with James Haas) of *Eucharistic Prayers for Children* published by Ave Maria Press. He has served as director of liturgy for the Archdiocese of Baltimore, vice chairperson of the Federation of Diocesan Liturgical Commissions and advisor to the Bishops' Committee on the Liturgy. Mr. Freburger lives with his wife, Mary, and son, William Daniel, in Kansas City, Missouri.

Acknowledgment:

Scripture readings used in this work are taken from the *Lectionary for Mass,* copyright © 1970 by the Confraternity of Christian Doctrine, Washington, D.C., and are used by license of said copyright owner.

No part of the *Lectionary for Mass* may be reproduced in any form without permission in writing. All rights reserved.

International Standard Book Number: 0-87793-309-X

Library of Congress Catalog Card Number: 83-72480

Printed and bound in the United States of America.

Contents

Easter Triduum and Easter Season

Ordinary Time

How to Use This Book

The scripture texts selected for THIS IS THE WORD OF THE LORD have been arranged for presentation by three readers. When the narrative involves more than three characters, the readers take more than one part. Character names are used when the reader represents only one person.

The readings are scripted for the three-person dialogue form. They are not intended to "match" any missalette or provide a speaking role for the congregation or choir. They may, of course, be adapted to include such parts if desired.

The complete text from the *Lectionary* is given. A much smoother presentation will result, however, if the material in brackets is omitted.

While the main emphasis is on the passion narratives and Holy Week, there is a wide selection of readings from the other seasons of the church year as well. These texts represent all three of the yearly cycles in the liturgical calendar.

This book presents an alternative—a different way of doing scripture proclamation. It is most effective when used sparingly. In that way it retains its freshness and helps fulfill the Vatican II mandate that "the treasures of the Bible are to be opened up more lavishly, so that richer fare may be provided for the faithful at the table of God's Word" (*Constitution on the Sacred Liturgy,* No. 51).

Introduction

One day, French author Jean Cocteau (1889-1963) returned after a long absence to the village he had grown up in. He remembered how he used to walk up the street from his home on the way to school, trailing his finger along the wall that bordered the sidewalk.

On this return visit, as an adult, he indulged in the same gesture but he found that it did not summon up for him any sense of his past. Suddenly, he realized he had been smaller then. So he bent down, closed his eyes and again traced the wall—but this time at the level of a little person.

Cocteau later wrote of the experience: "Just as the needle picks up the melody from the record, I obtained the melody of the past with my hand. I found everything: my cape, the leather of my satchel, the names of my friends and those of my teachers, certain expressions I had used, the sound of my grandfather's voice. . . ."

This is the way it is with us when we gather weekly in Christian community. We exercise our collective memory and discover the youth of our faith. We trail our finger along the foundations laid for us in the scriptures and we bring back the sights and sounds, the fears and triumphs, the faith and love that make us who we are. We accomplish this through the proclamation of the scriptures.

Sunday after Sunday, we are invited to identify with the stories of our forebears in the faith. The scriptures are dramatic. In a particular liturgical celebration, that drama may depend on the interpretative skill and reading ability of the individual lector or celebrant.

But there is the possibility of giving the dramatic element fuller expression by treating the text as a script. For example, the proclamation of the passion narratives in Holy Week by three readers has been an acceptable practice. From a utilitarian point of view, those lengthy texts almost demand such an arrangement. Even more to the point, so does the story they tell. The narratives of Jesus' suffering and death are the gospels' most dramatic parts.

This book adds to that basic repertoire by presenting another 85 scripture texts arranged for three readers, taken from the three-year cycle of readings in the lectionary. This selection highlights the "strong" seasons (Advent and Christmas, Lent and Easter) but it also includes a variety of readings from the ordinary time of the church year over the course of the three cycles. Some of these texts are so lengthy that the lectionary supplies a shorter version in addition to the complete one. I hope this book will render the proclamation of the unabridged passages more attractive.

Some liturgists object to this method of proclaiming the scriptures by dividing the texts into roles. We might indeed fault a weekly diet of scripture proclamation by several readers. But the purpose of this book is not to change our traditional ways of reading and proclaiming. It aims to offer parishes the choice of a different way for occasional use. Such variety can serve by contrast to keep the tradition fresh.

I would like to dedicate this book's revised and expanded edition to those countless men and women who have served as readers in our assemblies over the past two decades. May every reward promised in the scriptures they proclaimed be theirs!

—William J. Freburger

ADVENT AND CHRISTMAS SEASONS

Fourth Sunday of Advent

Year A/Lectionary no. 10

Isaiah 7:10-14
Matthew 1:18-24

ISAIAH Reading

Narrator: Again the Lord spoke to Ahaz:

Lord: Ask for a sign from the Lord, your God; let it be deep as the nether world, or high as the sky!

Narrator: But Ahaz answered,

Speaker: "I will not ask; I will not tempt the Lord!"

Narrator: Then he said:

Speaker: Listen, O house of David! Is it not enough for you to weary men, must you also weary my God? Therefore the Lord himself will give you this sign: the virgin shall be with child, and bear a son, and shall name him Immanuel.

Narrator: This the Word of the Lord.

MATTHEW Reading

Narrator: This is how the birth of Jesus Christ came about. When his mother Mary was engaged to Joseph, but before they lived together, she was found with child through the power of the Holy Spirit. Joseph her husband, an upright man unwilling to expose her to the law, decided to divorce her quietly. Such was his intention when suddenly the angel of the Lord appeared in a dream and said to him:

Speaker 1:   "Joseph, son of David, have no fear about taking Mary as your wife. It is by the Holy Spirit that she has conceived this child. She is to have a son and you are to name him Jesus because he will save his people from all their sins."

Narrator: All this happened to fulfill what the Lord had said through the prophet:

Speaker 2:   "The virgin shall be with child
and give birth to a son,
and they shall call him Emmanuel,"

Narrator: a name which means "God is with us." When Joseph awoke he did as the angel of the Lord had directed him and received her into his home as his wife.

This is the gospel of the Lord.

Fourth Sunday of Advent

(Years B and C are combined in one reading.)

Year B/Lectionary no. 11
Year C/Lectionary no. 12

Luke 1:26-38
Luke 1:39-45

Narrator: The angel Gabriel was sent from God to a town of Galilee named Nazareth, to a virgin betrothed to a man named Joseph, of the house of David. The virgin's name was Mary. Upon arriving, the angel said to her:

Speaker: "Rejoice, O highly favored daughter! The Lord is with you. Blessed are you among women."

Narrator: She was deeply troubled by his words, and wondered what his greeting meant. The angel went on to say to her:

Speaker: "Do not fear, Mary. You have found favor with God. You shall conceive and bear a son and give him the name Jesus. Great will be his dignity and he will be called Son of the Most High. The Lord God will give him the throne of David his father. He will rule over the house of Jacob and his reign will be without end."

Narrator: Mary said to the angel,

Mary: "How can this be since I do not know man?"

Narrator: The angel answered her:

Speaker: "The Holy Spirit will come upon you and the power of the Most High will overshadow you; hence, the holy offspring to be born will be called Son of God. Know that Elizabeth your kinswoman has conceived a son in her old age; she who was thought to be sterile is now in her sixth month, for nothing is impossible with God."

Mary:	[Mary said:] "I am the maidservant of the Lord. Let it be done to me as you say."
Narrator:	With that the angel left her.
	Thereupon Mary set out, proceeding in haste into the hill country to a town of Judah, where she entered Zechariah's house and greeted Elizabeth. When Elizabeth heard Mary's greeting, the baby stirred in her womb. Elizabeth was filled with the Holy Spirit, and cried out in a loud voice:
Speaker:	"Blessed are you among women and blessed is the fruit of your womb. But who am I that the mother of my Lord should come to me? The moment your greeting sounded in my ears, the baby stirred in my womb for joy. Blessed is she who trusted that the Lord's words to her would be fulfilled."
Narrator:	This is the gospel of the Lord.

Christmas, Masses at Midnight and Dawn

(The gospel readings for the Christmas Masses at midnight and dawn are combined.)

Years A, B, C/Lectionary no. 14
Years A, B, C/Lectionary no. 15

Luke 2:1-14
Luke 2:15-20

Reader 1: In those days Caesar Augustus published a decree ordering a census of the whole world.

Reader 2: This first census took place while Quirinius was governor of Syria. Everyone went to register, each to his own town.

Reader 3: And so Joseph went from the town of Nazareth in Galilee to Judea, to David's town of Bethlehem—because he was of the house and lineage of David—to register with Mary, his espoused wife, who was with child.

Reader 2: While they were there the days of her confinement were completed. She gave birth to her first-born son and wrapped him in swaddling clothes and laid him in a manger, because there was no room for them in the place where travelers lodged.

Reader 1: There were shepherds in the locality, living in the fields and keeping night watch by turns over their flocks.

Reader 3: The angel of the Lord appeared to them as the glory of the Lord shone around them, and they were very much afraid. The angel said to them:

Reader 1: "You have nothing to fear! I come to proclaim good news to you—tidings of great joy to be shared by the whole people. This day in David's city a savior has been born to you, the Messiah and Lord. Let this be a sign to you: in a manger you will find an infant wrapped in swaddling clothes."

All Readers: "Glory to God in high heaven,
                  peace on earth to those on whom his favor rests."

Reader 1:   When the angels had returned to heaven, the shepherds said to one another:

Reader 2:   "Let us go over to Bethlehem and see this event which the Lord has made known to us."

Reader 3:   They went in haste and found Mary and Joseph, and the baby lying in the manger;

Reader 1:   Once they saw, they understood what had been told them concerning this child. All who heard of it were astonished at the report given them by the shepherds.

Reader 3:   Mary treasured all these things and reflected on them in her heart.

Reader 2:   The shepherds returned, glorifying and praising God for all they had heard and seen, in accord with what had been told them.

Reader 1:   This is the gospel of the Lord.

Christmas, Mass During the Day

Years A, B, C/Lectionary no. 16

John 1:1-18

Reader 1:   In the beginning was the Word;

Reader 2:   the Word was in God's presence,

Reader 3:   and the Word was God.
He was present to God in the beginning.

Reader 2:   Through him all things came into being,
and apart from him nothing came to be.

Reader 3:   Whatever came to be in him, found life,
life for the light of men.

Reader 1:   The light shines on in darkness,
a darkness that did not overcome it.

Reader 3:   There was a man named John sent by God, who came as a witness to testify to the light, so that through him all men might believe—but only to testify to the light, for he himself was not the light. The real light which gives light to every man was coming into the world.

Reader 2:   He was in the world,
and through him the world was made,
yet the world did not know who he was.

Reader 3:   To his own he came,
yet his own did not accept him.

Reader 1:   Any who did accept him
he empowered to become children of God.

These are they who believe in his name—who were begotten not by blood, nor by carnal desire, nor by man's willing it, but by God.

Reader 2:	The Word became flesh and made his dwelling among us, and we have seen his glory: the glory of an only Son coming from the Father, filled with enduring love.
Reader 3:	John testified to him by proclaiming, "This is he of whom I said, 'The one who comes after me ranks ahead of me, for he was before me.' "
Reader 1:	Of his fullness we have all had a share— love following upon love.
Reader 2:	For while the law was a gift through Moses, this enduring love came through Jesus Christ.
Reader 3:	No one has ever seen God.
Reader 1:	It is God the only Son, ever at the Father's side, who has revealed him.
Reader 2:	This is the gospel of the Lord.

Holy Family

(The order of the three readings has been changed for continuity.)

Years A, B, C/Lectionary no. 17

Sirach 3:2-6,12-14
A: Matthew 2:13-15,19-23
B: Luke 2:22-40
C: Luke 2:41-52
Colossians 3:12-21

SIRACH Reading

Reader 1: The Lord sets a father in honor over his children;
a mother's authority he confirms over her sons.

Reader 2: He who honors his father atones for sins;
he stores up riches who reveres his mother.
He who honors his father is gladdened by children,
and when he prays he is heard.

Reader 3: He who reveres his father will live a long life;
he obeys the Lord who brings comfort to his mother.

Reader 2: My son, take care of your father when he is old;
grieve him not as long as he lives.

Reader 1: Even if his mind fail, be considerate with him;
revile him not in the fullness of your strength.

Reader 3: For kindness to a father will not be forgotten,
it will serve as a sin offering—it will take lasting root.

[Year A]

GOSPEL Reading

Reader 1: After the astrologers had left, the angel of the Lord
suddenly appeared in a dream to Joseph with the
command:

Reader 3:　"Get up, take the child and his mother, and flee to Egypt. Stay there until I tell you otherwise. Herod is searching for the child to destroy him."

Reader 2:　Joseph got up and took the child and his mother and left that night for Egypt. He stayed there until the death of Herod, to fulfill what the Lord had said through the prophet:

"Out of Egypt I have called my son."

Reader 1:　But after Herod's death, the angel of the Lord appeared in a dream to Joseph in Egypt with the command:

Reader 3:　"Get up, take the child and his mother, and set out for the land of Israel. Those who had designs on the life of the child are dead."

Reader 2:　He got up, took the child and his mother, and returned to the land of Israel. He heard, however, that Archelaus had succeeded his father Herod as king of Judea, and he was afraid to go back there.

Reader 1:　Instead, because of a warning received in a dream, Joseph went to the region of Galilee. There he settled in a town called Nazareth. In this way what was said through the prophets was fulfilled:

"He shall be called a Nazorean."

[Year B]

Reader 1:　When the day came to purify them according to the law of Moses, Mary and Joseph brought Jesus up to Jerusalem so that he could be presented to the Lord, for it is written in the law of the Lord, "Every first-born male shall be consecrated to the Lord." They came to offer in sacrifice "a pair of turtledoves or two young pigeons," in accord with the law of the Lord.

Reader 3: There lived in Jerusalem at the time a certain man named Simeon. He was just and pious, and awaited the consolation of Israel, and the Holy Spirit was upon him. It was revealed to him by the Holy Spirit that he would not experience death until he had seen the Anointed of the Lord.

Reader 2: He came to the temple now, inspired by the Spirit; and when the parents brought in the child Jesus to perform for him the customary ritual of the law, he took him in his arms and blessed God in these words:

Reader 1: "Now, Master, you can dismiss your servant in peace; you have fulfilled your word.
For my eyes have witnessed your saving deed displayed for all the people to see:
A revealing light to the Gentiles, the glory of your people Israel."

Reader 3: The child's father and mother were marveling at what was being said about him. Simeon blessed them and said to Mary his mother:

Reader 1: "This child is destined to be the downfall and the rise of many in Israel, a sign that will be opposed—and you yourself shall be pierced with a sword—so that the thoughts of many hearts may be laid bare."

Reader 2: There was also a certain prophetess, Anna by name, daughter of Phanuel of the tribe of Asher. She had seen many days, having lived seven years with her husband after her marriage and then as a widow until she was eight-four.

Reader 3: She was constantly in the temple, worshiping day and night in fasting and prayer. Coming on the scene at this moment, she gave thanks to God and talked about the child to all who looked forward to the deliverance of Jerusalem.

Reader 1: When the pair had fulfilled all the prescriptions of the law of the Lord, they returned to Galilee and their own town of Nazareth. The child grew in size and strength, filled with wisdom, and the grace of God was upon him.

Reader 1:   The parents of Jesus used to go every year to Jerusalem for the feast of Passover, and when he was twelve they went up for the celebration as was their custom.

Reader 3:   As they were returning at the end of the feast, the child Jesus remained behind unknown to his parents. Thinking he was in the party, they continued their journey for a day, looking for him among their relatives and acquaintances. Not finding him, they returned to Jerusalem in search of him.

Reader 2:   On the third day they came upon him in the temple sitting in the midst of the teachers, listening to them and asking them questions. All who heard him were amazed at his intelligence and his answers.

Reader 1:   When his parents saw him they were astonished, and his mother said to him:

Reader 2:   "Son, why have you done this to us? You see that your father and I have been searching for you in sorrow."

Reader 3:   [He said to them:] "Why did you search for me? Did you not know that I had to be in my Father's house?"

Reader 1:   But they did not grasp what he said to them. He went down with them, and came to Nazareth, and was obedient to them.

Reader 2:   His mother meanwhile kept all these things in memory. Jesus, for his part, progressed steadily in wisdom and age and grace before God and men.

[All Years]

COLOSSIANS Reading

Reader 1:   Because you are God's chosen ones, holy and beloved, clothe yourselves with heartfelt mercy, with kindness, humility, meekness, and patience.

Reader 2:   Bear with one another;

Reader 3:   forgive whatever grievances you have against one another.

Reader 2:   Forgive as the Lord has forgiven you.

Reader 3:   Over all these virtues put on love, which binds the rest together and makes them perfect.

Reader 1:   Christ's peace must reign in your hearts, since as members of one body you have been called to that peace.

Reader 2:   Dedicate yourselves to thankfulness.

Reader 3:   Let the word of Christ, rich as it is, dwell in you. In wisdom made perfect, instruct and admonish one another.

Reader 1:   Sing gratefully to God from your hearts in psalms, hymns, and inspired songs.

Reader 2:   Whatever you do, whether in speech or in action, do it in the name of the Lord Jesus. Give thanks to God the Father through him.

Reader 3:   You who are wives, be submissive to your husbands. This is your duty in the Lord.

Reader 1:   Husbands, love your wives. Avoid any bitterness toward them.

Reader 3:   You children, obey your parents in everything as the acceptable way in the Lord.

Reader 2:   And fathers, do not nag your children lest they lose heart. This is the Word of the Lord.

Baptism of the Lord

(The three readings are interwoven into one continuous reading.)

Years A, B, C/Lectionary no. 21

Acts 10:34-38
A: Matthew 3:13-17
B: Mark 1:7-11
C: Luke 3:15-16,21-22
Isaiah 42:1-4,6-7

ACTS Reading

Reader 1: Peter addressed Cornelius and the people assembled at his house in these words:

Reader 2: "I begin to see how true it is that God shows no partiality. Rather, the man of any nation who fears God and acts uprightly is acceptable to him. This is the message he has sent to the sons of Israel, 'the good news of peace' proclaimed through Jesus Christ who is Lord of all. I take it you know what has been reported all over Judea about Jesus of Nazareth, beginning in Galilee with the baptism John preached; of the way God anointed him with the Holy Spirit and power. He went about doing good works and healing all who were in the grip of the devil, and God was with him."

ISAIAH Reading

Reader 1: Here is my servant whom I uphold,
　　my chosen one with whom I am pleased,
Upon whom I have put my spirit;
　　he shall bring forth justice to the nations,
Not crying out, not shouting,
　　not making his voice heard in the street.
A bruised reed he shall not break,
　　and a smoldering wick he shall not quench,
Until he establishes justice on the earth;
　　the coastlands will wait for his teaching.

GOSPEL Reading

Reader 3:   Jesus, coming from Galilee, appeared before John at the Jordan to be baptized by him. John tried to refuse him with the protest,

Reader 1:   "I should be baptized by you, yet you come to me!"

Reader 3:   Jesus answered,

Reader 2:   "Give in for now. We must do this if we would fulfill all of God's demands."

Reader 3:   So John gave in. After Jesus was baptized, he came directly out of the water. Suddenly the sky opened and he saw the Spirit of God descend like a dove and hover over him. With that, a voice from the heavens said,

Reader 2:   "This is my beloved Son. My favor rests on him."

[Year B]

Reader 3:   The theme of John's preaching was:

Reader 1:   "One more powerful than I is to come after me. I am not fit to stoop and untie his sandal straps. I have baptized you in water; he will baptize you in the Holy Spirit."

Reader 3:   During that time, Jesus came from Nazareth in Galilee and was baptized in the Jordan by John. Immediately on coming up out of the water he saw the sky rent in two and the Spirit descending on him like a dove. Then a voice came from the heavens:

Reader 2:   "You are my beloved Son. On you my favor rests."

[Year C]

Reader 3:   The people were full of anticipation, wondering in their hearts whether John might be the Messiah. John answered them all by saying:

Reader 1:   "I am baptizing you in water, but there is one to come who is mightier than I. I am not fit to loosen his sandal strap. He will baptize you in the Holy Spirit and in fire."

Reader 3:   When all the people were baptized, and Jesus was at prayer after likewise being baptized, the skies opened and the Holy Spirit descended on him in visible form like a dove. A voice from heaven was heard to say,

Reader 2:   "You are my beloved Son. On you my favor rests."

[All Years]

ISAIAH Reading, cont.

Reader 1:   I, the Lord, have called you for the victory of justice,
              I have grasped you by the hand;
          I formed you, and set you
              as a covenant of the people,
              a light for the nations,
          To open the eyes of the blind,
              to bring out prisoners from confinement,
              and from the dungeon, those who live in darkness.

Reader 2:   This is the Word of the Lord.

LENTEN SEASON

First Sunday of Lent

Year A/Lectionary no. 22

Genesis 2:7-9; 3:1-7
Matthew 4:1-11

GENESIS Reading

Narrator: The Lord God formed man out of the clay of the ground and blew into his nostrils the breath of life, and so man became a living being. Then the Lord God planted a garden in Eden, in the east, and he placed there the man whom he had formed. Out of the ground the Lord God made various trees grow that were delightful to look at and good for food, with the tree of life in the middle of the garden and the tree of the knowledge of good and bad. Now the serpent was the most cunning of all the animals that the Lord God had made. The serpent asked the woman,

Serpent: "Did God really tell you not to eat from any of the trees in the garden?"

Woman: [The woman answered the serpent:] "We may eat of the fruit of the trees in the garden; it is only about the fruit of the tree in the middle of the garden that God said, 'You shall not eat it or even touch it, lest you die.' "

Serpent: [But the serpent said to the woman:] "You certainly will not die! No, God knows well that the moment you eat of it you will be like gods who know what is good and what is bad."

Narrator: The woman saw that the tree was good for food, pleasing to the eyes, and desirable for gaining wisdom. So she took some of the fruit and ate it; and she also gave some to her husband, who was with her, and he ate it. Then the eyes of both of them were opened, and they realized that they were naked; so they sewed fig leaves together and made loincloths for themselves.

This is the Word of the Lord.

MATTHEW Reading

Narrator: Jesus was led into the desert by the Spirit to be tempted by the devil. He fasted forty days and forty nights, and afterward was hungry. The tempter approached and said to him,

Devil: "If you are the Son of God, command these stones to turn into bread."

Jesus: [Jesus replied,] "Scripture has it:

'Not on bread alone is man to live
but on every utterance that comes from the mouth of God.' "

Narrator: Next the devil took him to the holy city, set him on the parapet of the temple, and said,

Devil: "If you are the Son of God, throw yourself down.
Scripture has it:

'He will bid his angels take care of you;
with their hands they will support you
that you may never stumble on a stone.' "

Jesus: [Jesus answered him,] "Scripture also has it:
'You shall not put the Lord your God to the test.' "

Narrator: The devil then took him to a lofty mountain peak and displayed before him all the kingdoms of the world in their magnificence, promising,

Devil: "All these will I bestow on you if you prostrate yourself in homage before me."

Jesus: [At this, Jesus said to him,] "Away with you, Satan!
Scripture says:

'You shall do homage to the Lord your God;
him alone shall you adore.' "

Narrator: At that the devil left him, and angels came and waited on him.

This is the gospel of the Lord.

First Sunday of Lent

Year C/Lectionary no. 24

Deuteronomy 26:4-10
Luke 4:1-13

DEUTERONOMY Reading

Reader 1:   Moses told the people:

Reader 2:   "The priest shall then receive the basket from you and shall set it in front of the altar of the Lord, your God. Then you shall declare before the Lord, your God,

Reader 3:   'My father was a wandering Aramean who went down to Egypt with a small household and lived there as an alien. But there he became a nation great, strong, and numerous.

Reader 1:   'When the Egyptians maltreated and oppressed us, imposing hard labor upon us, we cried to the Lord, the God of our fathers, and he heard our cry and saw our affliction, our toil and our oppression. He brought us out of Egypt with his strong hand and outstretched arm, with terrifying power, with signs and wonders;

Reader 3:   'and bringing us into this country, he gave us this land flowing with milk and honey. Therefore, I have now brought you the first fruits of the products of the soil which you, O Lord, have given me.'

Reader 2:   "And having set them before the Lord, your God, you shall bow down in his presence. Then you and your family, together with the Levite and the aliens who live among you, shall make merry over all these good things which the Lord, your God, has given you."

Reader 1:   This is the Word of the Lord.

LUKE Reading

Narrator: Jesus, full of the Holy Spirit, returned from the Jordan and was led by the Spirit into the desert for forty days, where he was tempted by the devil. During that time he ate nothing, and at the end of it he was hungry. The devil said to him,

Devil: "If you are the Son of God, command this stone to turn into bread."

Jesus: [Jesus answered him,] "Scripture has it, 'Not on bread alone shall man live.' "

Narrator: Then the devil took him up higher and showed him all the kingdoms of the world in a single instant. He said to him,

Devil: "I will give you all this power and the glory of these kingdoms; the power has been given to me and I give it to whomever I wish. Prostrate yourself in homage before me, and it shall all be yours."

Jesus: [In reply, Jesus said to him,] "Scripture has it,
    'You shall do homage to the Lord your God;
    him alone shall you adore.' "

Narrator: Then the devil led him to Jerusalem, set him on the parapet of the temple, and said to him,

Devil: "If you are the Son of God, throw yourself down from here, for Scripture has it,
    'He will bid his angels watch over you';
and again,
    'With their hands they will support you,
    that you may never stumble on a stone.' "

Jesus: [Jesus said to him in reply,] "It also says, 'You shall not put the Lord your God to the test.' "

Narrator: When the devil had finished all this tempting he left him, to await another opportunity.
This is the gospel of the Lord.

Second Sunday of Lent

Year B/Lectionary no. 26

Genesis 22:1-2,9,10-13,15-18
Mark 9:2-10

GENESIS Reading

Narrator: God put Abraham to the test [He called to him, "Abraham!" "Ready!" he replied. Then] God said:

God: "Take your son Isaac, your only one, whom you love, and go to the land of Moriah. There you shall offer him up as a holocaust on a height that I will point out to you."

Narrator: When they came to the place of which God had told him, Abraham built an altar there and arranged the wood on it. Then he reached out and took the knife to slaughter his son. But the Lord's messenger called to him from heaven,

Speaker: "Abraham, Abraham!"

Narrator: "Yes, Lord," he answered.

Speaker: "Do not lay your hand on the boy," [said the messenger]. "Do not do the least thing to him. I know now how devoted you are to God, since you did not withhold from me your own beloved son."

Narrator: As Abraham looked about, he spied a ram caught by its horns in the thicket. So he went and took the ram and offered it up as a holocaust in place of his son. Again the Lord's messenger called to Abraham from heaven and said:

Speaker: "I swear by myself, declares the Lord, that because you acted as you did in not withholding from me your beloved son, I will bless you abundantly and make your descendants as countless as the stars of the sky and the sands of the seashore; your descendants shall take possession of the gates of their enemies, and in your descendants all the nations of the earth shall find blessing—all this because you obeyed my command."

Narrator: This is the Word of the Lord.

MARK Reading

Narrator: Jesus took Peter, James and John off by themselves with him and led them up a high mountain. He was transfigured before their eyes and his clothes became dazzlingly white—whiter than the work of any bleacher could make them. Elijah appeared to them along with Moses; the two were in conversation with Jesus. Then Peter spoke to Jesus:

Peter: "Rabbi, how good it is for us to be here. Let us erect three booths on this site, one for you, one for Moses, and one for Elijah."

Narrator: He hardly knew what to say, for they were all overcome with awe. A cloud came, overshadowing them, and out of the cloud a voice:

God: "This is my Son, my beloved. Listen to him."

Narrator: Suddenly looking around they no longer saw anyone with them—only Jesus. As they were coming down the mountain, he strictly enjoined them not to tell anyone what they had seen before the Son of Man had risen from the dead. They kept this word of his to themselves, though they continued to discuss what "to rise from the dead" meant.

     This is the gospel of the Lord.

Third Sunday of Lent

(This gospel reading for year A may be used in place of those for years B and C.)

Year A (B,C)/Lectionary no. 28

John 4:5-42

Narrator: Jesus had to pass through Samaria, and his journey brought him to a Samaritan town named Shechem near the plot of land which Jacob had given to his son Joseph. This was the site of Jacob's well. The hour was about noon. When a Samaritan woman came to draw water, Jesus said to her,

Jesus: "Give me a drink."

Narrator: (His disciples had gone off to the town to buy provisions.) The Samaritan woman said to him,

Woman: "You are a Jew. How can you ask me, a Samaritan and a woman, for a drink?"

Narrator: (Recall that Jews have nothing to do with Samaritans.) Jesus replied:

Jesus: "If only you recognized God's gift,
and who it is that is asking you for a drink,
you would have asked him instead,
and he would have given you living water."

Woman: "Sir, [" she challenged him, "] you do not have a bucket and this well is deep. Where do you expect to get this flowing water? Surely you do not pretend to be greater than our ancestor Jacob, who gave us this well and drank from it with his sons and his flocks?"

Narrator: Jesus replied,

Jesus:	"Everyone who drinks this water will be thirsty again. But whoever drinks the water I give him will never be thirsty; no, the water I give shall become the fountain within him, leaping up to provide eternal life."
Narrator:	The woman said to him,
Woman:	"Give me this water, sir, so that I shall not grow thirsty and have to keep coming here to draw water."
Jesus:	[He said to her,] "Go, call your husband, and then come back here."
Woman:	"I have no husband," [replied the woman.]
Jesus:	"You are right in saying you have no husband! ["] Jesus exclaimed. "] The fact is, you have had five, and the man you are living with now is not your husband. What you said is true."
Woman:	"Sir, ["] answered the woman, "] I can see you are a prophet. Our ancestors worshiped on this mountain, but you people claim that Jerusalem is the place where men ought to worship God."
Narrator:	Jesus told her,
Jesus:	"Believe me, woman, an hour is coming when you will worship the Father neither on this mountain nor in Jerusalem. You people worship what you do not understand, while we understand what we worship; after all, salvation is from the Jews. Yet an hour is coming, and is already here, when authentic worshipers will worship the Father in Spirit and truth. Indeed, it is just such worshipers

the Father seeks.
God is Spirit,
and those who worship him
must worship him in Spirit and truth.''

Narrator: The woman said to him:

Woman: "I know there is a Messiah coming."

Narrator: (This term means Anointed.)

Woman: "When he comes, he will tell us everything."

Narrator: Jesus replied,

Jesus: "I who speak to you am he."

Narrator: His disciples, returning at this point, were surprised that Jesus was speaking with a woman. No one put a question, however, such as "What do you want of him?" or "Why are you talking with her?" The woman then left her water jar and went off into the town. She said to the people:

Woman: "Come and see someone who told me everything I ever did! Could this not be the Messiah?"

Narrator: At that they set out from town to meet him. Meanwhile, the disciples were urging him, "Rabbi, eat something." But he told them:

Jesus: "I have food to eat
of which you do not know."

Narrator: At this the disciples said to one another, "Do you suppose that someone has brought him something to eat?" Jesus explained to them:

Jesus: "Doing the will of him who sent me
and bringing his work to completion
is my food.
Do you not have a saying:
'Four months more

and it will be harvest!''?
Listen to what I say:
Open your eyes and see!
The fields are shining for harvest!
The reaper already collects his wages
and gathers a yield for eternal life,
that sower and reaper may rejoice together.
Here we have the saying verified:
'One man sows; another reaps.'
I sent you to reap
what you had not worked for.
Others have done the labor,
and you have come into their gain.''

Narrator: Many Samaritans from that town believed in him on the strength of the woman's word of testimony: ''He told me everything I ever did.'' The result was that, when these Samaritans came to him, they begged him to stay with them awhile. So he stayed there two days, and through his own spoken word many more came to faith. As they told the woman: ''No longer does our faith depend on your story. We have heard for ourselves, and we know that this really is the Savior of the world.''

This is the gospel of the Lord.

Fourth Sunday of Lent

(This gospel reading for year A may be used in place of those for years B and C.)

Year A (B,C)/Lectionary no. 31

John 9:1-41

Narrator:	As Jesus walked along, he saw a man who had been blind from birth. His disciples asked him,
Speaker 1:	"Rabbi, was it his sin or that of his parents that caused him to be born blind?"
Speaker 2:	"Neither, ['' answered Jesus: '']

       It was no sin, either of this man
       or of his parents.
       Rather, it was to let God's works show forth in him.
       We must do the deeds of him who sent me
       while it is day.
       The night comes on
       when no one can work.
       While I am in the world
       I am the light of the world."

Narrator:	With that Jesus spat on the ground, made mud with his saliva, and smeared the man's eyes with the mud. Then he told him,
Speaker 2:	"Go, wash in the pool of Siloam."
Narrator:	(This name means "One who has been sent.") So the man went off and washed, and came back able to see. His neighbors and the people who had been accustomed to see him begging began to ask,
Speaker 1:	"Isn't this the fellow who used to sit and beg?"
Narrator:	Some were claiming it was he; others maintained it was not but someone who looked like him. The man himself said,

Speaker 2:	"I am the one."
Speaker 1:	[They said to him then,] "How were your eyes opened?"
Speaker 2:	[He answered:] "That man they call Jesus made mud and smeared it on my eyes, telling me to go to Siloam and wash. When I did go and wash, I was able to see."
Speaker 1:	"Where is he?" [they asked.]
Speaker 2:	[He replied,] "I have no idea."
Narrator:	Next, they took the man who had been born blind to the Pharisees. (Note that it was on a sabbath that Jesus had made the mud paste and opened his eyes.) The Pharisees, in turn, began to inquire how he had recovered his sight. He told them,
Speaker 2:	"He put mud on my eyes. I washed it off, and now I can see."
Narrator:	This prompted some of the Pharisees to assert,
Speaker 1:	"This man cannot be from God because he does not keep the sabbath."
Narrator:	Others objected, "If a man is a sinner, how can he perform signs like these?" They were sharply divided over him. Then they addressed the blind man again:
Speaker 1:	"Since it was your eyes he opened, what do you have to say about him?"
Speaker 2:	"He is a prophet," [he replied.]
Narrator:	The Jews refused to believe that he had really been born blind and had begun to see, until they summoned the parents of this man who could now see.
Speaker 1:	"Is this your son? [" they asked, "] and if so, do you attest that he was blind at birth? How do you account for the fact that now he can see?"

Narrator:	The parents answered: "We know this is our son, and we know he was blind at birth. But how he can see now, or who opened his eyes, we have no idea. Ask him. He is old enough to speak for himself." (His parents answered in this fashion because they were afraid of the Jews, who had already agreed among themselves that anyone who acknowledged Jesus as the Messiah would be put out of the synagogue. That was why his parents said, "He is of age—ask him.") A second time they summoned the man who had been born blind and said to him,
Speaker 1:	"Give glory to God! First of all, we know this man is a sinner."
Speaker 2:	"I do not know whether he is a sinner or not, [" he answered. "] I know this much: I was blind before; now I can see."
Speaker 1:	[They persisted:] "Just what did he do to you? How did he open your eyes?"
Speaker 2:	"I have told you once, but you would not listen to me, [" he answered them. "] Why do you want to hear it all over again? Do not tell me you want to become his disciples too?"
Narrator:	They retorted scornfully:
Speaker 1:	"You are the one who is that man's disciple. We are disciples of Moses. We know that God spoke to Moses, but we have no idea where this man comes from."
Narrator:	He came back at them:
Speaker 2:	"Well, this is news! You do not know where he comes from, yet he opened my eyes. We know that God does not hear sinners, but that if someone is devout and obeys his will, he listens to him. It is unheard of that anyone ever gave sight to a person blind from birth. If this man were not from God, he could never have done such a thing."

Speaker 1:	"What! ["] they exclaimed, "] You are steeped in sin from your birth, and you are giving us lectures?"
Narrator:	With that they threw him out bodily. When Jesus heard of his expulsion, he sought him out and asked him,
Speaker 1:	"Do you believe in the Son of Man?"
Speaker 2:	[He answered,] "Who is he, sir, that I may believe in him?"
Speaker 1:	"You have seen him, ["] Jesus replied. "] He is speaking to you now."
Speaker 2:	"I do believe, Lord," [he said,]
Narrator:	and he bowed down to worship him. Then Jesus said:
Speaker 1:	"I came into this world to divide it to make the sightless see and the seeing blind."
Narrator:	Some of the Pharisees around him picked this up, saying, "You are not calling us blind, are you?" To which Jesus replied:
Speaker 1:	"If you were blind there would be no sin in that. 'But we see,' you say, and your sin remains."
Narrator:	This is the gospel of the Lord.

Fifth Sunday of Lent

(This gospel reading for year A may be used in place of those for years B and C.)

Year A (B,C)/Lectionary no. 34

John 11:1-45

Narrator: There was a certain man named Lazarus who was sick. He was from Bethany, the village of Mary and her sister Martha. (This Mary whose brother Lazarus was sick was the one who anointed the Lord with perfume and dried his feet with her hair.) The sisters sent word to Jesus to inform him, "Lord, the one you love is sick." Upon hearing this, Jesus said:

Jesus: "This sickness is not to end in death;
rather it is for God's glory,
that through it the Son of God may be glorified."

Narrator: Jesus loved Martha and her sister and Lazarus very much. Yet, after hearing that Lazarus was sick, he stayed on where he was for two days more. Finally, he said to his disciples,

Jesus: "Let us go back to Judea."

Speaker: "Rabbi, ["] protested the disciples, ["] with the Jews only recently trying to stone you, you are going back up there again?"

Narrator: Jesus answered:

Jesus: "Are there not twelve hours of daylight?
If a man goes walking by day he does not stumble
because he sees the world bathed in light.
But if he goes walking at night he will stumble
since there is no light in him."

[After uttering these words, he added,] "Our beloved Lazarus has fallen asleep, but I am going there to wake him."

44

Narrator:	At this the disciples objected,
Speaker:	"Lord, if he is asleep his life will be saved."
Narrator:	Jesus had been speaking about his death, but they thought he meant sleep in the sense of slumber. Finally Jesus said plainly:
Jesus:	"Lazarus is dead. For your sakes I am glad I was not there, that you may come to believe. In any event, let us go to him."
Narrator:	Then Thomas (the name means "Twin") said to his fellow disciples,
Speaker:	"Let us go along, to die with him."
Narrator:	When Jesus arrived at Bethany, he found that Lazarus had already been in the tomb four days. The village was not far from Jerusalem—just under two miles—and many Jewish people had come out to console Martha and Mary over their brother. When Martha heard that Jesus was coming, she went to meet him, while Mary sat at home. Martha said to Jesus:
Speaker:	"Lord, if you had been here, my brother would never have died. Even now, I am sure that God will give you whatever you ask of him."
Jesus:	"Your brother will rise again," [Jesus assured her.]
Speaker:	"I know he will rise again, [" Martha replied, "] in the resurrection on the last day."
Narrator:	Jesus told her:
Jesus:	"I am the resurrection and the life: whoever believes in me, though he should die, will come to life; and whoever is alive and believes in me will never die. Do you believe this?"

Speaker:	"Yes, Lord, [" she replied. "] I have come to believe that you are the Messiah, the Son of God: he who is to come into the world."
Narrator:	When she had said this she went back and called her sister Mary.
Speaker:	"The Teacher is here, asking for you," [she whispered.]
Narrator:	As soon as Mary heard this, she got up and started out in his direction. (Actually Jesus had not yet come into the village but was still at the spot where Martha had met him.) The Jews who were in the house with Mary consoling her saw her get up quickly and go out, so they followed her, thinking she was going to the tomb to weep there. When Mary came to the place where Jesus was, seeing him, she fell at his feet and said to him,
Speaker:	"Lord, if you had been here my brother would never have died."
Narrator:	When Jesus saw her weeping, and the Jews who had accompanied her also weeping, he was troubled in spirit, moved by the deepest emotions.
Jesus:	"Where have you laid him?" [he asked.]
Speaker:	"Lord, come and see," [they said.]
Narrator:	Jesus began to weep, which caused the Jews to remark, "See how much he loved him!" But some said,
Speaker:	"He opened the eyes of that blind man. Why could he not have done something to stop this man from dying?"
Narrator:	Once again troubled in spirit, Jesus approached the tomb. It was a cave with a stone laid across it.
Jesus:	"Take away the stone," [Jesus directed.]
Narrator:	Martha, the dead man's sister, said to him,

Speaker:	"Lord, it has been four days now; surely there will be a stench!"
Jesus:	[Jesus replied,] "Did I not assure you that if you believed, you would see the glory of God displayed?"
Narrator:	They then took away the stone and Jesus looked upward and said:
Jesus:	"Father, I thank you for having heard me. I know that you always hear me but I have said this for the sake of the crowd, that they may believe that you sent me."
Narrator:	Having said this, he called loudly,
Jesus:	"Lazarus, come out!"
Narrator:	The dead man came out bound head and foot with linen strips, his face wrapped in a cloth.
Jesus:	"Untie him, [" Jesus told them, "] and let him go free."
Narrator:	This caused many of the Jews who had come to visit Mary, and had seen what Jesus did, to put their faith in him.
	This is the gospel of the Lord.

Passion (Palm) Sunday

Year A/Lectionary no. 38

Matthew 26:14-27:66

Narrator: The Passion of our Lord Jesus Christ according to Matthew.

One of the Twelve whose name was Judas Iscariot went off to the chief priests and said,

Speaker: "What are you willing to give me if I hand Jesus over to you?"

Narrator: They paid him thirty pieces of silver, and from that time on he kept looking for an opportunity to hand him over. On the first day of the feast of Unleavened Bread, the disciples came up to Jesus and said,

Speaker: "Where do you wish us to prepare the Passover supper for you?"

Jesus: [He said,] "Go to this man in the city and tell him, 'The Teacher says, My appointed time draws near. I am to celebrate the Passover with my disciples in your house.' "

Narrator: The disciples then did as Jesus had ordered, and prepared the Passover supper. When it grew dark he reclined at table with the Twelve. In the course of the meal he said,

Jesus: "I give you my word, one of you is about to betray me."

Narrator: Distressed at this, they began to say to him one after another,

Speaker: "Surely it is not I, Lord?"

Jesus: [He replied:] "The man who has dipped his hand into the dish with me is the one who will hand me over. The Son of Man is departing, as Scripture says of him, but woe to that man by whom the Son of Man is betrayed. Better for him if he had never been born.''

Narrator: Then Judas, his betrayer, spoke:

Speaker: "Surely it is not I, Rabbi?''

Jesus: [Jesus answered,] "It is you who have said it.''

Narrator: During the meal Jesus took bread, blessed it, broke it, and gave it to his disciples.

Jesus: "Take this and eat it, ['' he said, "] this is my body.''

Narrator: Then he took a cup, gave thanks, and gave it to them.

Jesus: "All of you must drink from it, ['' he said, "] for this is my blood, the blood of the covenant, to be poured out in behalf of many for the forgiveness of sins. I tell you, I will not drink this fruit of the vine from now until the day I drink new wine with you in my Father's reign.''

Narrator: Then after singing songs of praise, they walked out to the Mount of Olives. Jesus then said to them,

Jesus: "Tonight your faith in me will be shaken, for Scripture has it:

    'I will strike the shepherd
    and the sheep of the flock will be dispersed.'

But after I am raised up, I will go to Galilee ahead of you.''

Narrator: Peter responded,

Speaker: "Though all may have their faith in you shaken, mine will never be shaken!''

Jesus: [Jesus said to him,] "I give you my word, before the cock crows tonight you will deny me three times.''

Speaker: [Peter replied,] "Even though I have to die with you, I will never disown you.''

Narrator:	And all the other disciples said the same. Then Jesus went with them to a place called Gethsemani. He said to his disciples,
Jesus:	"Stay here while I go over there and pray."
Narrator:	He took along Peter and Zebedee's two sons, and began to experience sorrow and distress. Then he said to them,
Jesus:	"My heart is nearly broken with sorrow. Remain here and stay awake with me."
Narrator:	He advanced a little and fell prostrate in prayer.
Jesus:	"My Father, if it is possible, let this cup pass me by. Still, let it be as you would have it, not as I."
Narrator:	When he returned to his disciples, he found them asleep. He said to Peter,
Jesus:	"So you could not stay awake with me for even an hour? Be on guard, and pray that you may not undergo trial. The spirit is willing but nature is weak."
Narrator:	Withdrawing a second time, he began to pray:
Jesus:	"My Father, if this cannot pass me by without my drinking it, your will be done!"
Narrator:	Once more, on his return, he found them asleep; they could not keep their eyes open. He left them again, withdrew somewhat, and began to pray a third time, saying the same words as before. Finally he returned to his disciples and said to them,
Jesus:	"Sleep on now. Enjoy your rest! The hour is on us when the Son of Man is to be handed over to the power of evil men. Get up! Let us be on our way! See, my betrayer is here."
Narrator:	While he was still speaking, Judas, one of the Twelve, arrived accompanied by a great crowd with swords and

clubs. They had been sent by the chief priests and elders of the people. His betrayer had arranged to give them a signal, saying,

Speaker: "The man I shall embrace is the one; take hold of him."

Narrator: He immediately went over to Jesus, said to him,

Speaker: "Peace, Rabbi,"

Narrator: and embraced him. Jesus answered,

Jesus: "Do what you are here for, friend!"

Narrator: At that moment they stepped forward to lay hands on Jesus, and arrested him. Suddenly one of those who accompanied Jesus put his hand to his sword, drew it, and slashed at the high priest's servant, cutting off his ear. Jesus said to him:

Jesus: "Put back your sword where it belongs. Those who use the sword are sooner or later destroyed by it. Do you not suppose I can call on my Father to provide at a moment's notice more than twelve legions of angels? But then how would the Scriptures be fulfilled which say it must happen this way?"

Narrator: At that very time Jesus said to the crowd:

Jesus: "Am I a brigand, that you have come armed with swords and clubs to arrest me? From day to day I sat teaching in the temple precincts, yet you never arrested me. Nonetheless, all this has happened in fulfillment of the writings of the prophets."

Speaker: Then all the disciples deserted him and fled. Those who had apprehended Jesus led him off to Caiaphas, the high priest, where the scribes and elders were convened. Peter kept following him at a distance as far as the high priest's residence. Going inside, he sat down with the guards to see the outcome.

Narrator:	The chief priests, with the whole Sanhedrin, were busy trying to obtain false testimony against Jesus so that they might put him to death. They discovered none, despite the many false witnesses who took the stand. Finally two came forward who stated:
Speaker:	"This man has declared, 'I can destroy God's sanctuary and rebuild it in three days.' "
Narrator:	The high priest rose to his feet and addressed him:
Speaker:	"Have you no answer to the testimony leveled against you?"
Narrator:	But Jesus remained silent. The high priest then said to him:
Speaker:	"I order you to tell us under oath before the living God whether you are the Messiah, the Son of God."
Jesus:	[Jesus answered:] "It is you who say it. But I tell you this: Soon you will see the Son of Man seated at the right hand of the Power and coming on the clouds of heaven."
Narrator:	At this the high priest tore his robes:
Speaker:	"He has blasphemed! What further need have we of witnesses? Remember, you heard the blasphemy. What is your verdict?"
Narrator:	They answered, "He deserves death!" Then they began to spit in his face and hit him. Others slapped him, saying:
Speaker:	"Play the prophet for us, Messiah! Who struck you?"
Narrator:	Peter was sitting in the courtyard when one of the serving girls came over to him and said, "You too were with Jesus the Galilean." He denied it in front of everyone:
Speaker:	"I don't know what you are talking about!"
Narrator:	When he went out to the gate another girl saw him and said to those nearby, "This man was with Jesus the Nazorean." Again he denied it with an oath:

Speaker:	"I don't know the man!"
Narrator:	A little while later some bystanders came over to Peter and said, "You are certainly one of them! Even your accent gives you away!" At that he began cursing and swore,
Speaker:	"I don't even know the man!"
Narrator:	Just then a rooster began to crow and Peter remembered the prediction Jesus had made: "Before the rooster crows you will three times disown me." He went out and began to weep bitterly.

At daybreak all the chief priests and the elders of the people took formal action against Jesus to put him to death. They bound him and led him away to be handed over to the procurator Pilate. Then Judas, who had handed him over, seeing that Jesus had been condemned, began to regret his action deeply. He took the thirty pieces of silver back to the chief priests and elders and said, |
Speaker:	"I did wrong to deliver up an innocent man!"
Narrator:	They retorted, "What is that to us? It is your affair!" So Judas flung the money into the temple and left. He went off and hanged himself. The chief priests picked up the silver, observing,
Speaker:	"It is not right to deposit this in the temple treasury since it is blood money."
Narrator:	After consultation, they used it to buy the potter's field as a cemetery for foreigners. That is why that field, even today, is called Blood Field. On that occasion, what was said through Jeremiah the prophet was fulfilled: "They took the thirty pieces of silver, the value of a man with a price on his head, a price set by the Israelites, and they paid it out for the potter's field just as the Lord had commanded me." Jesus was arraigned before the procurator, who questioned him:
Speaker:	"Are you the king of the Jews?"

Jesus:	[Jesus responded,] "As you say."
Narrator:	Yet when he was accused by the chief priests and elders, he had made no reply. Then Pilate said to him,
Speaker:	"Surely you hear how many charges they bring against you?"
Narrator:	He did not answer him on a single count, much to the procurator's surprise. Now on the occasion of a festival the procurator was accustomed to release one prisoner, whom the crowd would designate. They had at the time a notorious prisoner named Barabbas. Since they were already assembled, Pilate said to them,
Speaker:	"Which one do you wish me to release for you, Barabbas or Jesus, the so-called Messiah?"
Narrator:	He knew, of course, that it was out of jealousy that they had handed him over. While he was still presiding on the bench, his wife sent him a message:
Speaker:	"Do not interfere in the case of that holy man. I had a dream about him today which has greatly upset me."
Narrator:	Meanwhile, the chief priests and elders convinced the crowds that they should ask for Barabbas and have Jesus put to death. So when the procurator asked them,
Speaker:	"Which one do you wish me to release for you?"
Narrator:	[They said,] "Barabbas."
Speaker:	[Pilate said to them,] "Then what am I to do with Jesus, the so-called Messiah?"
Narrator:	"Crucify him!" [they all cried.]
Speaker:	[He said,] "Why, what crime has he committed?"
Narrator:	But they only shouted the louder, "Crucify him!" Pilate finally realized that he was making no impression and that

a riot was breaking out instead. He called for water and washed his hands in front of the crowd, declaring as he did so,

Speaker: "I am innocent of the blood of this just man. The responsibility is yours."

Narrator: The whole people said in reply, "Let his blood be on us and our children."

At that, he released Barabbas to them. Jesus, however, he first had scourged; then he handed him over to be crucified. The procurator's soldiers took Jesus inside the praetorium and collected the whole cohort around him. They stripped off his clothes and wrapped him in a scarlet military cloak. Weaving a crown out of thorns they fixed it on his head, and stuck a reed in his right hand. They they began to mock him by dropping to their knees before him, saying,

Speaker: "All hail, king of the Jews!"

Narrator: They also spat at him. Afterward they took hold of the reed and kept striking him on the head. Finally, when they had finished making a fool of him, they stripped him of the cloak, dressed him in his own clothes, and led him off to crucifixion. On their way out they met a Cyrenian named Simon. This man they pressed into service to carry the cross. Upon arriving at a site called Golgotha (a name which means Skull Place), they gave him a drink of wine flavored with gall, which he tasted but refused to drink.

Speaker: When they had crucified him, they divided his clothes among them by casting lots; then they sat down there and kept watch over him. Above his head they had put the charge against him in writing: "THIS IS JESUS, KING OF THE JEWS." Two insurgents were crucified along with him, one at his right and one at his left.

Narrator: People going by kept insulting him, tossing their heads and saying:

Speaker:	"So you are the one who was going to destroy the temple and rebuild it in three days! Save yourself, why don't you? Come down off that cross if you are God's Son!"
Narrator:	The chief priests, the scribes and the elders also joined in the jeering:
Speaker:	"He saved others but he cannot save himself! So he is the king of Israel! Let's see him come down from that cross, then we will believe in him. He relied on God; let God rescue him now if he wants to. After all, he claimed, 'I am God's Son.' "
Narrator:	The insurgents who had been crucified with him kept taunting him in the same way. From noon onward, there was darkness over the whole land until midafternoon. Then toward midafternoon Jesus cried out in a loud tone,
Jesus:	*"Eli, Eli, lema sabachthani?* [" that is, "] My God, my God, why have you forsaken me?"
Narrator:	This made some of the bystanders who heard it remark,
Speaker:	"He is invoking Elijah!"
Narrator:	Immediately one of them ran off and got a sponge. He soaked it in cheap wine, and sticking it on a reed, tried to make him drink. Meanwhile, the rest said,
Speaker:	"Leave him alone. Let's see whether Elijah comes to his rescue."
Narrator:	Once again Jesus cried out in a loud voice, and then gave up his spirit.

(Pause)

Suddenly the curtain of the sanctuary was torn in two from top to bottom. Many bodies of saints who had fallen asleep were raised. After Jesus' resurrection they came forth from their tombs and entered the holy city and appeared to many. The centurion and his men who were keeping watch over Jesus were terror-stricken at seeing the earthquake and all that was happening, and said,

Speaker: "Clearly this was the Son of God!"

Narrator: Many women were present looking on from a distance. They had followed Jesus from Galilee to attend to his needs.

Speaker: Among them were Mary Magdalene, and Mary the mother of James and Joseph, and the mother of Zebedee's sons.

Narrator: When evening fell, a wealthy man from Arimathea arrived, Joseph by name. He was another of Jesus' disciples, and had gone to request the body of Jesus. Thereupon Pilate issued an order for its release.

Speaker: Taking the body, Joseph wrapped it in fresh linen and laid it in his own new tomb which had been hewn from a formation of rock. Then he rolled a huge stone across the entrance of the tomb and went away. But Mary Magdalene and the other Mary remained sitting there, facing the tomb.

Narrator: The next day, the one following the Day of Preparation, the chief priests and the Pharisees called at Pilate's residence.

Speaker: "Sir, ['' they said, ''] we have recalled that that impostor while he was still alive made the claim, 'After three days I will rise.' You should issue an order having the tomb kept under surveillance until the third day. Otherwise his disciples may go and steal him and tell the people, 'He has been raised from the dead!' This final imposture would be worse than the first."

Narrator: Pilate told them, "You have a guard. Go and secure the tomb as best you can." So they went and kept it under the surveillance of the guard, after fixing a seal to the stone.

This is the gospel of the Lord.

Passion (Palm) Sunday

Year B/Lectionary no. 38

Mark 14:1-15:47

Narrator:	The Passion of our Lord Jesus Christ according to Mark.
	The feasts of Passover and Unleavened Bread were to be observed in two days' time, and therefore the chief priests and scribes began to look for a way to arrest Jesus by some trick and kill him. Yet they pointed out,
Speaker:	"Not during the festival, or the people may riot."
Narrator:	When Jesus was in Bethany reclining at table in the house of Simon the leper, a woman entered carrying an alabaster jar of perfume made from expensive aromatic nard. Breaking the jar, she began to pour the perfume on his head. Some were saying to themselves indignantly:
Speaker:	"What is the point of this extravagant waste of perfume? It could have been sold for over three hundred silver pieces and the money given to the poor."
Narrator:	They were infuriated at her. But Jesus said:
Jesus:	"Let her alone. Why do you criticize her? She has done me a kindness. The poor you will always have with you and you can be generous to them whenever you wish, but you will not always have me. She has done what she could. By perfuming my body, she is anticipating its preparation for burial. I assure you, wherever the good news is proclaimed throughout the world, what she has done will be told in her memory."
Narrator:	Then Judas Iscariot, one of the Twelve, went off to the chief priests to hand Jesus over to them. Hearing what he had to say, they were jubilant and promised to give him money. He for his part kept looking for an opportune way to hand him over.

On the first day of Unleavened Bread, when it was customary to sacrifice the paschal lamb, his disciples said to him,

Speaker: "Where do you wish us to go to prepare the Passover supper for you?"

Narrator: He sent two of his disciples with these instructions:

Jesus: "Go into the city and you will come upon a man carrying a water jar. Follow him. Whatever house he enters, say to the owner, 'The Teacher asks, Where is my guestroom where I may eat the Passover with my disciples?' Then he will show you an upstairs room, spacious, furnished, and all in order. That is the place you are to get ready for us."

Narrator: The disciples went off. When they reached the city they found it just as he had told them, and they prepared the Passover supper. As it grew dark he arrived with the Twelve. They reclined at table, and in the course of the meal Jesus said,

Jesus: "I give you my word, one of you is about to betray me, yes, one who is eating with me."

Narrator: They began to say to him sorrowfully, one by one,

Speaker: "Surely not I!"

Jesus: [He said,] "It is one of the Twelve—a man who dips into the dish with me. The Son of Man is going the way the Scripture tells of him. Still, accursed be that man by whom the Son of Man is betrayed. It were better for him had he never been born."

Narrator: During the meal he took bread, blessed and broke it, and gave it to them.

Jesus: "Take this, [" he said, "] this is my body."

Narrator: He likewise took a cup, gave thanks, and passed it to them, and they all drank from it.

Jesus:	[He said to them:] "This is my blood, the blood of the covenant, to be poured out on behalf of many. I solemnly assure you, I will never again drink of the fruit of the vine until the day when I drink it in the reign of God."
Narrator:	After singing songs of praise, they walked out to the Mount of Olives. Jesus then said to them:

Jesus:	"Your faith in me shall be shaken, for Scripture has it,
	
	   'I will strike the shepherd
	   and the sheep will be dispersed.'
	
	But after I am raised up, I will go to Galilee ahead of you."

Narrator:	Peter said to him,
Speaker:	"Even though all are shaken in faith, it will not be that way with me."
Jesus:	[Jesus answered,] "I give you my assurance, this very night before the cock crows twice, you will deny me three times."
Narrator:	But Peter kept reasserting vehemently,
Speaker:	"Even if I have to die with you, I will not disown you."
Narrator:	They all said the same. They went then to a place named Gethsemani.
Jesus:	"Sit down here while I pray," [he said to his disciples;]
Narrator:	at the same time he took along with him Peter, James, and John. Then he began to be filled with fear and distress. He said to them,
Jesus:	"My heart is filled with sorrow to the point of death. Remain here and stay awake."
Narrator:	He advanced a little and fell to the ground, praying that if it were possible this hour might pass him by. He kept saying,

60

Jesus:	"*Abba* (O Father), you have the power to do all things. Take this cup away from me. But let it be as you would have it, not as I."
Narrator:	When he returned he found them asleep. He said to Peter,
Jesus:	"Asleep, Simon? You could not stay awake for even an hour? Be on guard and pray that you may not be put to the test. The spirit is willing but nature is weak."
Narrator:	Going back again he began to pray in the same words. Once again he found them asleep on his return. They could not keep their eyes open, nor did they know what to say to him. He returned a third time and said to them,
Jesus:	"Still sleeping? Still taking your ease? It will have to do. The hour is on us. You will see that the Son of Man is to be handed over into the clutches of evil men. Rouse yourselves and come along. See! My betrayer is near."
Narrator:	Even while he was still speaking, Judas, one of the Twelve, made his appearance accompanied by a crowd with swords and clubs; these people had been sent by the chief priests, the scribes, and the elders. The betrayer had arranged a signal for them, saying,
Speaker:	"The man I shall embrace is the one; arrest him and lead him away, taking every precaution."
Narrator:	He then went directly over to him and said, "Rabbi!" and embraced him. At this they laid hands on him and arrested him. One of the bystanders drew his sword and struck the high priest's slave, cutting off his ear. Addressing himself to them, Jesus said,
Jesus:	"You have come out to arrest me armed with swords and clubs as if against a brigand. I was within your reach daily, teaching in the temple precincts, yet you never arrested me. But now, so that the Scriptures may be fulfilled. . . ."

Narrator: With that, all deserted him and fled. There was a young man following him who was covered by nothing but a linen cloth. As they seized him he left the cloth behind and ran off naked.

Speaker: Then they led Jesus off to the high priest, and all the chief priests, the elders and the scribes came together. Peter followed him at a distance right into the high priest's courtyard, where he found a seat with the temple guard and began to warm himself at the fire.

Narrator: The chief priests with the whole Sanhedrin were busy soliciting testimony against Jesus that would lead to his death, but they could not find any. Many spoke against him falsely under oath but their testimony did not agree. Some, for instance, on taking the stand, testified falsely by alleging,

Speaker: "We heard him declare, 'I will destroy this temple made by human hands,' and 'In three days I will construct another not made by human hands.' "

Narrator: Even so, their testimony did not agree. The high priest rose to his feet before the court and began to interrogate Jesus:

Speaker: "Have you no answer to what these men testify against you?"

Narrator: But Jesus remained silent; he made no reply. Once again the high priest interrogated him:

Speaker: "Are you the Messiah, the Son of the Blessed One?"

Jesus: [Then Jesus answered:] "I am; and you will see the Son of Man seated at the right hand of the Power and coming with the clouds of heaven."

Narrator: At that the high priest tore his robes and said:

Speaker: "What further need do we have of witnesses? You have heard the blasphemy. What is your verdict?"

Narrator:	They all concurred in the verdict "guilty," with its sentence of death. Some of them then began to spit on him. They blindfolded him and hit him, saying, "Play the prophet!" while the officers manhandled him. While Peter was down in the courtyard, one of the servant girls of the high priest came along. When she noticed Peter warming himself, she looked more closely at him and said, "You too were with Jesus of Nazareth." But he denied it:
Speaker:	"I don't know what you are talking about! What are you getting at?"
Narrator:	Then he went out into the gateway. At that moment a rooster crowed. The servant girl, keeping an eye on him, started again to tell the bystanders, "This man is one of them."
	Once again he denied it. A little later the bystanders said to Peter once more, "You are certainly one of them! You're a Galilean, are you not?"
	He began to curse, and to swear,
Speaker:	"I don't even know the man you are talking about!"
Narrator:	Just then a second cockcrow was heard and Peter recalled the prediction Jesus had made to him, "Before the cock crows twice you will disown me three times." He broke down and began to cry.
Speaker:	As soon as it was daybreak the chief priests, with the elders and the scribes (that is, the whole Sanhedrin), reached a decision.
Narrator:	They bound Jesus, led him away, and handed him over to Pilate. Pilate interrogated him:
Speaker:	"Are you the king of the Jews?"
Jesus:	"You are the one who is saying it," [Jesus replied.]
Narrator:	The chief priests, meanwhile, brought many accusations against him. Pilate interrogated him again:

Speaker:	"Surely you have some answer? See how many accusations they are leveling against you."
Narrator:	But greatly to Pilate's surprise, Jesus made no further response. Now on the occasion of a festival he would release for them one prisoner—any man they asked for. There was a prisoner named Barabbas jailed along with the rebels who had committed murder in the uprising. When the crowd came up to press their demand that he honor the custom, Pilate rejoined,
Speaker:	"Do you want me to release the king of the Jews for you?"
Narrator:	He was aware, of course, that it was out of jealousy that the chief priests had handed him over. Meanwhile, the chief priests incited the crowd to have him release Barabbas instead. Pilate again asked them,
Speaker:	"What am I to do with the man you call the king of the Jews?"
Narrator:	They shouted back, "Crucify him!" Pilate protested,
Speaker:	"Why? What crime has he committed?"
Narrator:	They only shouted the louder, "Crucify him!" So Pilate, who wished to satisfy the crowd, released Barabbas to them, and after he had had Jesus scourged, he handed him over to be crucified.
Speaker:	The soldiers now led Jesus away into the hall known as the praetorium; at the same time they assembled the whole cohort. They dressed him in royal purple, then wove a crown of thorns and put it on him, and began to salute him, "All hail! King of the Jews!" Continually striking Jesus on the head with a reed and spitting at him, they genuflected before him and pretended to pay him homage.
Narrator:	When they had finished mocking him, they stripped him of the purple, dressed him in his own clothes, and led him out to crucify him. A man named Simon of Cyrene, the father of Alexander and Rufus, was coming in from the fields and they pressed him into service to carry the cross.

Speaker: When they brought Jesus to the site of Golgotha (which means "Skull Place"), they tried to give him wine drugged with myrrh, but he would not take it. Then they crucified him and divided up his garments by rolling dice for them to see what each should take.

Narrator: It was about nine in the morning when they crucified him. The inscription proclaiming his offense read, "THE KING OF THE JEWS." With him they crucified two insurgents, one at his right and one at his left. People going by kept insulting him, tossing their heads and saying,

Speaker: "Ha, ha! So you were going to destroy the temple and rebuild it in three days! Save yourself now by coming down from that cross!"

Narrator: The chief priests and the scribes also joined in and jeered:

Speaker: "He saved others but he cannot save himself! Let the 'Messiah,' the 'king of Israel,' come down from that cross here and now so that we can see it and believe in him!"

Narrator: The men who had been crucified with him likewise kept taunting him. When noon came, darkness fell on the whole countryside and lasted until midafternoon. At that time Jesus cried in a loud voice,

Jesus: *"Eloi, Eloi, lama sabachthani?* ["* which means, "] My God, my God, why have you forsaken me?"

Narrator: A few of the bystanders who heard it remarked,

Speaker: "Listen! He is calling on Elijah!"

Narrator: Someone ran off, and soaking a sponge in sour wine, stuck it on a reed to try to make him drink. The man said,

Speaker: "Now let's see whether Elijah comes to take him down."

Narrator: Then Jesus, uttering a loud cry, breathed his last.

(Pause)

At that moment the curtain in the sanctuary was torn in two from top to bottom. The centurion who stood guard over him on seeing the manner of his death, declared,

Speaker: "Clearly this man was the Son of God!"

Narrator: There were also women present looking on from a distance. Among them were Mary Magdalene, Mary the mother of James the younger and Joses, and Salome. These women had followed Jesus when he was in Galilee and attended to his needs. There were also many others who had come up with him to Jerusalem.

Speaker: As it grew dark (it was Preparation Day, that is, the eve of the sabbath), Joseph from Arimathea arrived—a distinguished member of the Sanhedrin. He was another who looked forward to the reign of God. He was bold enough to seek an audience with Pilate, and urgently requested the body of Jesus.

Narrator: Pilate was surprised that Jesus should have died so soon. He summoned the centurion and inquired whether Jesus was already dead. Learning from him that he was dead, Pilate released the corpse to Joseph. Then, having bought a linen shroud, Joseph took him down, wrapped him in the linen, and laid him in a tomb which had been cut out of rock. Finally he rolled a stone across the entrance of the tomb. Meanwhile, Mary Magdalene and Mary the mother of Joses observed where he had been laid.

This is the gospel of the Lord.

Passion (Palm) Sunday

Year C/Lectionary no. 38

Luke 22:14-23:56

Narrator:	The Passion of our Lord Jesus Christ according to Luke.
	When the hour arrived, Jesus took his place at table, and the apostles with him. He said to them:
Jesus:	"I have greatly desired to eat this Passover with you before I suffer. I tell you, I will not eat again until it is fulfilled in the kingdom of God."
Narrator:	Then taking a cup he offered a blessing in thanks and said:
Jesus:	"Take this and divide it among you; I tell you, from now on I will not drink of the fruit of the vine until the coming of the reign of God."
Narrator:	Then taking bread and giving thanks, he broke it and gave it to them, saying:
Jesus:	"This is my body to be given for you. Do this as a remembrance of me."
Narrator:	He did the same with the cup after eating, saying as he did so:
Jesus:	"This cup is the new covenant in my blood, which will be shed for you. And yet the hand of my betrayer is with me at this table. The Son of Man is following out his appointed course, but woe to that man by whom he is betrayed."
Narrator:	Then they began to dispute among themselves as to which of them would do such a deed. A dispute arose among them about who would be regarded as the greatest.

Jesus:	[He said:] "Earthly kings lord it over their people. Those who exercise authority over them are called their benefactors. Yet it cannot be that way with you. Let the greater among you be as the junior, the leader as the servant. Who, in fact, is the greater—he who reclines at table or he who serves the meal? Is it not the one who reclines at table? Yet I am in your midst as the one who serves you. You are the ones who have stood loyally by me in my temptations. I for my part assign to you the dominion my Father has assigned to me. In my kingdom, you will eat and drink at my table, and you will sit on thrones judging the twelve tribes of Israel. Simon, Simon! Remember that Satan has asked for you to sift you all like wheat. But I have prayed for you that your faith may never fail. You in turn must strengthen your brothers."
Speaker:	"Lord, [" he said to him,"] at your side I am prepared to face imprisonment and death itself."
Jesus:	[Jesus replied,] "I tell you, Peter, the rooster will not crow today until you have three times denied that you know me."
Narrator:	He asked them,
Jesus:	"When I sent you on mission without purse or traveling bag or sandals, were you in need of anything?"
Speaker:	"Not a thing," [they replied.]
Jesus:	[He said to them:] "Now, however, the man who has a purse must carry it; the same with the traveling bag. And the man without a sword must sell his coat and buy one. It is written in Scripture, 'He was counted among the wicked,' and this, I tell you, must come to be fulfilled in me. All that has to do with me approaches its climax."
Speaker:	[They said,] "Lord, here are two swords!"
Jesus:	[He answered,] "Enough."

Narrator:	Then he went out and made his way, as was his custom, to the Mount of Olives; his disciples accompanied him. On reaching the place he said to them,
Jesus:	"Pray that you may not be put to the test."
Narrator:	He withdrew from them about a stone's throw, then went down on his knees and prayed in these words:
Jesus:	"Father, if it is your will, take this cup from me; yet not my will but yours be done."
Narrator:	An angel then appeared to him from heaven to strengthen him. In his anguish he prayed with all the greater intensity, and his sweat became like drops of blood falling to the ground. Then he rose from prayer and came to his disciples, only to find them asleep, exhausted with grief. He said to them,
Jesus:	"Why are you sleeping? Wake up, and pray that you may not be subjected to the trial."
Narrator:	While he was still speaking a crowd came, led by the man named Judas, one of the Twelve. He approached Jesus to embrace him. Jesus said to him,
Jesus:	"Judas, would you betray the Son of Man with a kiss?"
Narrator:	When the companions of Jesus saw what was going to happen, they said,
Speaker:	"Lord, shall we use the sword?"
Narrator:	One of them went so far as to strike the high priest's servant and cut off his right ear. Jesus said in answer to their question,
Jesus:	"Enough!"
Narrator:	Then he touched the ear and healed the man. But to those who had come out against him—the chief priests, the chiefs of the temple guard, and the ancients—Jesus said,

Jesus:	"Am I a criminal that you come out after me armed with swords and clubs? When I was with you day after day in the temple you never raised a hand against me. But this is your hour—the triumph of darkness!"
Narrator:	They led him away under arrest and brought him to the house of the high priest, while Peter followed at a distance. Later they lighted a fire in the middle of the courtyard and were sitting beside it, and Peter sat among them. A servant girl saw him sitting in the light of the fire. She gazed at him intently, then said, "This man was with him." He denied the fact, saying,
Speaker:	"Woman, I do not know him."
Narrator:	A little while later someone else saw him and said, "You are one of them too." But Peter said,
Speaker:	"No, sir, not I!"
Narrator:	About an hour after that another spoke more insistently: "This man was certainly with him, for he is a Galilean." Peter responded,
Speaker:	"My friend, I do not know what you are talking about."
Narrator:	At the very moment he was saying this, a rooster crowed. The Lord turned around and looked at Peter, and Peter remembered the words that the Lord had spoken to him, "Before the rooster crows today you will deny me three times." He went out and wept bitterly. Meanwhile the men guarding Jesus amused themselves at his expense. They blindfolded him first, slapped him, and then taunted him:
Speaker:	"Play the prophet; which one struck you?"
Narrator:	And they directed many other insulting words at him. At daybreak, the council which was made up of the elders of the people, the chief priests, and the scribes, assembled again. Once they had brought him before their council, they said,

Speaker:	"Tell us, are you the Messiah?"
Jesus:	[He replied,] "If I tell you, you will not believe me, and if I question you, you will not answer. This much only will I say: 'From now on, the Son of Man will have his seat at the right hand of the Power of God.' "
Speaker:	"So you are the Son of God?" [they asked in chorus.]
Jesus:	[He answered,] "It is you who say I am."
Speaker:	[They said,] "What need have we of witnesses? We have heard it from his own mouth."
Narrator:	Then the entire assembly rose up and led him before Pilate. They started his prosecution by saying,
Speaker:	"We found this man subverting our nation, opposing the payment of taxes to Caesar, and calling himself the Messiah, a king."
Narrator:	Pilate asked him,
Speaker:	"Are you the king of the Jews?"
Jesus:	[He answered,] "That is your term."
Narrator:	Pilate reported to the chief priests and the crowds,
Speaker:	"I do not find a case against this man."
Narrator:	But they insisted, "He stirs up the people by his teaching throughout the whole of Judea, from Galilee, where he began, to this very place."
Speaker:	On hearing this Pilate asked if the man was a Galilean; and when he learned that he was under Herod's jurisdiction, he sent him to Herod, who also happened to be in Jerusalem at the time.
Narrator:	Herod was extremely pleased to see Jesus. From the reports about him he had wanted for a long time to see him, and

he was hoping to see him work some miracle. He questioned Jesus at considerable length, but Jesus made no answer. The chief priests and scribes were at hand to accuse him vehemently. Herod and his guards then treated him with contempt and insult, after which they put a magnificent robe on him and sent him back to Pilate. Herod and Pilate, who had previously been set against each other, became friends from that day. Pilate then called together the chief priests, the ruling class, and the people, and said to them:

Speaker: "You have brought this man before me as one who subverts the people. I have examined him in your presence and have no charge against him arising from your allegations. Neither has Herod, who therefore has sent him back to us; obviously this man has done nothing to deserve death. Therefore I mean to release him, once I have taught him a lesson."

Narrator: The whole crowd cried out, "Away with this man; release Barabbas for us!"

This Barabbas had been thrown in prison for causing an uprising in the city, and for murder. Pilate addressed them again, for he wanted Jesus to be the one he released. But they shouted back, "Crucify him, crucify him!" He said to them for the third time,

Speaker: "What wrong is this man guilty of? I have not discovered anything about him deserving the death penalty. I will therefore chastise him and release him."

Narrator: But they demanded with loud cries that he be crucified, and their shouts increased in violence. Pilate then decreed that what they demanded should be done. He released the one they asked for, who had been thrown in prison for insurrection and murder, and delivered Jesus up to their wishes. As they led him away, they laid hold of one Simon the Cyrenean who was coming in from the fields. They put a crossbeam on Simon's shoulder for him to carry along behind Jesus. A great crowd of people followed him, including women who beat their breasts and lamented over him. Jesus turned to them and said:

Jesus: "Daughters of Jerusalem, do not weep for me. Weep for yourselves and for your children. The days are coming when they will say, 'Happy are the sterile, the wombs that never bore and the breasts that never nursed.' Then they will begin saying to the mountains, 'Fall on us,' and to the hills, 'Cover us.' If they do these things in the green wood, what will happen in the dry?"

Narrator: Two others who were criminals were led along with him to be crucified. When they came to Skull Place, as it was called, they crucified him there and the criminals as well, one on his right and the other on his left. Jesus said,

Jesus: "Father, forgive them; they do not know what they are doing."

Narrator: They divided his garments, rolling dice of them. The people stood there watching, and the leaders kept jeering at him, saying,

Speaker: "He saved others; let him save himself if he is the Messiah of God, the chosen one."

Narrator: The soldiers also made fun of him, coming forward to offer him their sour wine and saying,

Speaker: "If you are the king of the Jews, save yourself."

Narrator: There was an inscription over his head:
"THIS IS THE KING OF THE JEWS."
One of the criminals hanging in crucifixion blasphemed him, "Aren't you the Messiah? Then save yourself and us." But the other one rebuked him:

Speaker: "Have you no fear of God, seeing you are under the same sentence? We deserve it, after all. We are only paying the price for what we've done, but this man has done nothing wrong. [" He then said, "] Jesus, remember me when you enter upon your reign."

Jesus: [And Jesus replied,] "I assure you: this day you will be with me in paradise."

Narrator: It was now around midday, and darkness came over the whole land until midafternoon with an eclipse of the sun. The curtain in the sanctuary was torn in two. Jesus uttered a loud cry and said,

Jesus: "Father, into your hands I commend my spirit."

Narrator: After he said this, he expired.

(Pause)

The centurion, upon seeing what had happened, gave glory to God by saying,

Speaker: "Surely this was an innocent man."

Narrator: After the crowd assembled for this spectacle witnessed what had happened, they returned beating their breasts.

All his friends and the women who had accompanied him from Galilee were standing at a distance watching everything. There was a man named Joseph, an upright and holy member of the Sanhedrin, who had not been associated with their plan or their action. He was from Arimathea, a Jewish town, and he looked expectantly for the reign of God. This man approached Pilate with a request for Jesus' body. He took it down, wrapped it in fine linen, and laid it in a tomb hewn out of the rock, in which no one had yet been buried. That was the day of Preparation, and the sabbath was about to begin. The women who had come with him from Galilee followed along behind. They saw the tomb and how his body was buried. Then they went back home to prepare spices and perfumes. They observed the sabbath as a day of rest, in accordance with the law.

This is the gospel of the Lord.

EASTER TRIDUUM
AND
EASTER SEASON

Holy Thursday, Mass of the Lord's Supper

(The three readings for Holy Thursday are arranged in one continuous reading.)

Years A, B, C/Lectionary no. 40

Exodus 12:1-8,11-14
John 13:1-15
1 Corinthians 11:23-26

Narrator: *Tonight we celebrate the Passover of the Lord, the mystery of our salvation that began when* the Lord said to Moses and Aaron in the land of Egypt,

Reader 1:   "This month shall stand at the head of your calendar; you shall reckon it the first month of the year. Tell the whole community of Israel: On the tenth of this month every one of your families must procure for itself a lamb, one apiece for each household. If a family is too small for a whole lamb, it shall join the nearest household in procuring one and shall share in the lamb in proportion to the number of persons who partake of it. The lamb must be a year-old male and without blemish. You may take it from either the sheep or the goats.

Reader 2:   "You shall keep it until the fourteenth day of this month, and then, with the whole assembly of Israel present, it shall be slaughtered during the evening twilight. They shall take some of its blood and apply it to the two doorposts and the lintel of every house in which they partake of the lamb. That same night they shall eat its roasted flesh with unleavened bread and bitter herbs.

Reader 1:   "This is how you are to eat it: with your loins girt, sandals on feet and your staff in hand, you shall eat like those who are in flight. It is the Passover of the Lord. For on this same night I will go through Egypt, striking down every first-born of the land, both man and beast, and executing judgment on all the gods of Egypt—I, the Lord!

Reader 2:	"But the blood will mark the houses where you are. Seeing the blood, I will pass over you; thus, when I strike the land of Egypt, no destructive blow will come upon you. This day shall be a memorial feast for you, which all your generations shall celebrate with pilgrimage to the Lord, as a perpetual institution."
Narrator:	*And so it was that* before the feast of Passover, Jesus realized that the hour had come for him to pass from this world to the Father. He had loved his own in the world, and would show his love for them to the end. The devil had already induced Judas, son of Simon Iscariot, to hand Jesus over;
Reader 1:	and so, during supper, Jesus—fully aware that he had come from God and was going to God, the Father who had handed everything over to him—rose from the meal and took off his cloak. He picked up a towel and tied it around himself. Then he poured water into a basin and began to wash his disciples' feet and dry them with the towel he had around him. Thus he came to Simon Peter, who said to him,
Narrator:	"Lord, are you going to wash my feet?"
Reader 2:	[Jesus answered,] "You may not realize now what I am doing, but later you will understand."
Narrator:	[Peter replied,] "You shall never wash my feet!"
Reader 2:	"If I do not wash you, [" Jesus answered, "] you shall have no share in my heritage."
Narrator:	"Lord, [" Simon Peter said to him, "] then not only my feet, but my hands and head as well."
Reader 2:	[Jesus told him,] "The man who has bathed has no need to wash except for his feet; he is entirely cleansed, just as you are; though not all."
Reader 1:	(The reason he said, "Not all are washed clean," was that he knew his betrayer.)

Narrator:	After he had washed their feet, he put his cloak back on and reclined at table once more. He said to them:
Reader 2:	"Do you understand what I just did for you? You address me as 'Teacher' and 'Lord,' and fittingly enough, for that is what I am. But if I washed your feet— I who am Teacher and Lord— then you must wash each other's feet. What I just did was to give you an example: as I have done, so you must do."
Reader 1:	*Later, the Apostle Paul would describe this Passover Meal by writing these words in his First Letter to the Corinthians:* I received from the Lord what I handed on to you, namely, that the Lord Jesus on the night in which he was betrayed took bread, and after he had given thanks, broke it and said,
Reader 2:	"This is my body, which is for you. Do this in rememberance of me."
Reader 1:	In the same way, after the supper, he took the cup, saying,
Reader 2:	"This cup is the new covenant in my blood. Do this, whenever you drink it, in remembrance of me."
Narrator:	Every time, then, you eat this bread and drink this cup, you proclaim the death of the Lord until he comes! This is the word of the Lord.

Good Friday

Years A, B, C/Lectionary no. 41

John 18:1-19:42

Narrator:	Jesus went out with his disciples across the Kidron valley. There was a garden there, and he and his disciples entered it. The place was familiar to Judas as well (the one who was to hand him over) because Jesus had often met there with his disciples. Judas took the cohort as well as guards supplied by the chief priests and the Pharisees, and came there with lanterns, torches, and weapons. Jesus, aware of all that would happen to him, stepped forward and said to them,
Jesus:	"Who is it you want?"
Speaker:	"Jesus the Nazorean," [they replied.]
Jesus:	"I am he," [he answered.]
Narrator:	(Now Judas, the one who was to hand him over, was there with them.) As Jesus said to them, "I am he," they retreated slightly and fell to the ground. Jesus put the question to them again,
Jesus:	"Who is it you want?"
Speaker:	"Jesus the Nazorean," [they repeated.]
Jesus:	"I have told you, I am he, [" Jesus said. "] If I am the one you want, let these men go."
Narrator:	(This was to fulfill what he had said, "I have not lost one of those you gave me.") Then Simon Peter, who had a sword, drew it and struck the slave of the high priest, severing his right ear. (The slave's name was Malchus.) At that Jesus said to Peter,

Jesus:	"Put your sword back in its sheath. Am I not to drink the cup the Father has given me?"
Narrator:	Then the soldiers of the cohort, their tribune, and the Jewish police arrested Jesus and bound him. They led him first to Annas, the father-in-law of Caiaphas who was high priest that year. (It was Caiaphas who had proposed to the Jews the advantage of having one man die for the people.) Simon Peter, in company with another disciple, kept following Jesus closely.
Speaker:	This disciple, who was known to the high priest, stayed with Jesus as far as the high priest's courtyard, while Peter was left standing at the gate. The disciple known to the high priest came out and spoke to the woman at the gate, and then brought Peter in. This servant girl who kept the gate said to Peter,
Narrator:	"Aren't you one of this man's followers?"
Speaker:	"Not I," [he replied.]
Narrator:	Now the night was cold, and the servants and the guards who were standing around had made a charcoal fire to warm themselves by. Peter joined them and stood there warming himself. The high priest questioned Jesus, first about his disciples, then about his teaching. Jesus answered by saying:
Jesus:	"I have spoken publicly to any who would listen. I always taught in a synagogue or in the temple area where all the Jews come together. There was nothing secret about anything I said.

"Why do you question me? Question those who heard me when I spoke. It should be obvious they will know what I said." |
| *Narrator:* | At this reply, one of the guards who was standing nearby gave Jesus a sharp blow on the face. |
| *Speaker:* | "Is that any way to answer the high priest?" [he said.] |

Jesus:	[Jesus replied,] "If I said anything wrong produce the evidence, but if I spoke the truth why hit me?"
Narrator:	Annas next sent him, bound, to the high priest Caiaphas.
Speaker:	All through this, Simon Peter had been standing there warming himself. They said to him,
Narrator:	"Are you not a disciple of his?"
Speaker:	[He denied:] "I am not!"
Narrator:	"But did I not see you with him in the garden?" insisted one of the high priest's slaves—as it happened, a relative of the man whose ear Peter had severed. Peter denied it again. At that moment a cock began to crow.
	At daybreak they brought Jesus from Caiaphas to the praetorium. They did not enter the praetorium themselves, for they had to avoid ritual impurity if they were to eat the Passover supper. Pilate came out to them.
Speaker:	"What accusation do you bring against this man?" [he demanded.]
Narrator:	"If he were not a criminal, [" they retorted, "] we would certainly not have handed him over to you."
Speaker:	[At this Pilate said,] "Why do you not take him and pass judgment on him according to your law?"
Narrator:	"We may not put anyone to death," [the Jews answered.]
	(This was to fulfill what Jesus had said, indicating the sort of death he would die). Pilate went back into the praetorium and summoned Jesus.
Speaker:	"Are you the King of the Jews?" [he asked him.]
Jesus:	[Jesus answered,] "Are you saying this on your own, or have others been telling you about me?"

Speaker:	"I am no Jew! ["" Pilate retorted."] It is your own people and the chief priests who have handed you over to me. What have you done?"
Jesus:	[Jesus answered:]
	"My kingdom does not belong to this world. If my kingdom were of this world, my subjects would be fighting to save me from being handed over to the Jews. As it is, my kingdom is not here."
Speaker:	[At this Pilate said to him,] "So, then, you are a king?"
Jesus:	[Jesus replied:]
	"It is you who say I am a king. The reason I was born, the reason why I came into the world, is to testify to the truth. Anyone committed to the truth hears my voice."
Speaker:	"Truth! ["" said Pilate, "] What does that mean?"
Narrator:	After this remark, Pilate went out again to the Jews and told them:
Speaker:	"Speaking for myself, I find no case against this man. Recall your custom whereby I release to you someone at Passover time. Do you want me to release to you the king of the Jews?"
Narrator:	[They shouted back,] "We want Barabbas, not this one!"
Speaker:	(Barabbas was an insurrectionist.) Pilate's next move was to take Jesus and have him scourged. The soldiers then wove a crown of thorns and fixed it on his head, throwing around his shoulders a cloak of royal purple. Repeatedly they came up to him and said, "All hail, King of the Jews!", slapping his face as they did so.
Narrator:	Pilate went out a second time and said to the crowd:

Speaker:	"Observe what I do. I am going to bring him out to you to make you realize that I find no case against him."
Narrator:	When Jesus came out wearing the crown of thorns and the purple cloak, Pilate said to them,
Speaker:	"Look at the man!"
Narrator:	As soon as the chief priests and the temple police saw him they shouted, "Crucify him! Crucify him!"
Speaker:	[Pilate said,] "Take him and crucify him yourselves; I find no case against him."
Narrator:	"We have our law, [" the Jews responded, "] and according to that law he must die because he made himself God's Son."
Speaker:	When Pilate heard this kind of talk, he was more afraid than ever.
Narrator:	Going back into the praetorium, he said to Jesus,
Speaker:	"Where do you come from?"
Narrator:	Jesus would not give him any answer.
Speaker:	"Do you refuse to speak to me?[" Pilate asked him."] Do you not know that I have the power to release you and the power to crucify you?"
Jesus:	[Jesus answered:] "You would have no power over me whatever unless it were given you from above. That is why he who handed me over to you is guilty of the greater sin."
Speaker:	After this, Pilate was eager to release him, but the Jews shouted,
Narrator:	"If you free this man you are no 'Friend of Caesar.' Anyone who makes himself a king becomes Caesar's rival."

Speaker:	Pilate heard what they were saying, then brought Jesus outside and took a seat on a judge's bench at the place called the Stone Pavement—*Gabbatha* in Hebrew. (It was the Preparation Day for Passover, and the hour was about noon.)
Narrator:	He said to the Jews,
Speaker:	"Look at your king!"
Narrator:	[At this they shouted,] "Away with him! Away with him! Crucify him!"
Speaker:	"What! ["]Pilate exclaimed,"] Shall I crucify your king?"
Narrator:	[The chief priests replied,] "We have no king but Caesar."
Speaker:	In the end, Pilate handed Jesus over to be crucified. Jesus was led away, and carrying the cross by himself, went out to what is called the Place of the Skull (in Hebrew, *Golgotha*).
Narrator:	There they crucified him, and two others with him: one on either side, Jesus in the middle. Pilate had an inscription placed on the cross which read, JESUS THE NAZOREAN THE KING OF THE JEWS
Speaker:	This inscription, in Hebrew, Latin and Greek, was read by many of the Jews, since the place where Jesus was crucified was near the city. The chief priests of the Jews tried to tell Pilate,
Narrator:	"You should not have written, 'The King of the Jews.' Write instead, 'This man claimed to be king of the Jews.' "
Speaker:	[Pilate answered,] "What I have written, I have written."
Narrator:	After the soldiers had crucified Jesus they took his garments and divided them four ways, one for each soldier.

There was also his tunic, but this tunic was woven in one piece from top to bottom and had no seam. They said to each other,

Speaker: "We shouldn't tear it. Let's throw dice to see who gets it."

Narrator: (The purpose of this was to have the Scripture fulfilled:

"They divided my garments among them; for my clothing they cast lots.")

And this was what the soldiers did. Near the cross of Jesus there stood his mother, his mother's sister, Mary the wife of Clopas, and Mary Magdalene. Seeing his mother there with the disciple whom he loved, Jesus said to his mother,

Jesus: "Woman, there is your son."

Narrator: In turn he said to the disciple,

Jesus: "There is your mother."

Narrator: From that hour onward, the disciple took her into his care. After that, Jesus, realizing that everything was now finished, to bring the Scripture to fulfillment said,

Jesus: "I am thirsty."

Narrator: There was a jar there, full of common wine. They stuck a sponge soaked in this wine on some hyssop and raised it to his lips. When Jesus took the wine, he said,

Jesus: "Now it is finished."

Narrator: Then he bowed his head, and delivered over his spirit. Since it was the Preparation Day the Jews did not want to have the bodies left on the cross during the sabbath, for that sabbath was a solemn feast day. They asked Pilate that the legs be broken and the bodies be taken away. Accordingly, the soldiers came and broke the legs of the men crucified with Jesus, first of one, then of the other. When they came to Jesus and saw that he was already dead, they did not break his legs. One of the soldiers ran a lance into his side, and immediately blood and water flowed out.

Speaker: (This testimony has been given by an eyewitness, and his testimony is true. He tells what he knows is true, so that you may believe.) These events took place for the fulfillment of Scripture:

"Break none of his bones."

There is still another Scripture passage which says:

"They shall look on him whom they have pierced."

Narrator: Afterward, Joseph of Arimathea, a disciple of Jesus (although a secret one for fear of the Jews), asked Pilate's permission to remove Jesus' body. Pilate granted it, so they came and took the body away. Nicodemus (the man who had first come to Jesus at night) likewise came, bringing a mixture of myrrh and aloes which weighed about a hundred pounds. They took Jesus' body, and in accordance with Jewish burial custom bound it up in wrappings of cloth with perfumed oils.

Speaker: In the place where he had been crucified there was a garden, and in the garden a new tomb in which no one had ever been laid. Because of the Jewish Preparation Day they laid Jesus there, for the tomb was close at hand.

Narrator: This is the gospel of the Lord.

Easter Vigil

Years A, B, C/Lectionary no. 42-1

Genesis 1:1-2:2

READING ONE

Reader 1:   In the beginning, when God created the heavens and the earth, the earth was a formless wasteland, and darkness covered the abyss, while a mighty wind swept over the waters. Then God said,

Reader 2:   "Let there be light,"

Reader 1:   and there was light. God saw how good the light was.

Reader 3:   God then separated the light from the darkness. God called the light "day," and darkness he called "night."

Reader 1:   Thus evening came and morning followed—the first day.

Reader 2:   Then God said, "Let there be a dome in the middle of the waters, to separate one body of water from the other."

Reader 3:   And so it happened: God made the dome, and it separated the water above the dome from the water below it. God called the dome "the sky."

Reader 1:   Evening came, and morning followed—the second day.

Reader 2:   Then God said, "Let the water under the sky be gathered into a single basin, so that the dry land may appear."

Reader 1:   And so it happened: the water under the sky was gathered into its basin, and the dry land appeared. God called the dry land "the earth," and the basin of the water he called "the sea." God saw how good it was.

Reader 2:	Then God said, "Let the earth bring forth vegetation: every kind of plant that bears seed and every kind of fruit tree on earth that bears fruit with its seed in it."
Reader 3:	And so it happened: the earth brought forth every kind of plant that bears seed and every kind of fruit tree on earth that bears fruit with its seed in it. God saw how good it was.
Reader 1:	Evening came, and morning followed—the third day.
Reader 2:	Then God said: "Let there be lights in the dome of the sky, to separate day from night. Let them mark the fixed times, the days and the years, and serve as luminaries in the dome of the sky, to shed light upon the earth."
Reader 3:	And so it happened: God made the two great lights, the greater one to govern the day, and the lesser one to govern the night; and he made the stars. God set them in the dome of the sky, to shed light upon the earth, to govern the day and the night, and to separate the light from the darkness. God saw how good it was.
Reader 1:	Evening came, and morning followed—the fourth day.
Reader 2:	Then God said, "Let the water teem with an abundance of living creatures, and on the earth let birds fly beneath the dome of the sky."
Reader 3:	And so it happened: God created the great sea monsters and all kinds of swimming creatures with which the water teems, and all kinds of winged birds.
Reader 1:	God saw how good it was, and God blessed them, saying,
Reader 2:	"Be fertile, multiply, and fill the water of the seas; and let the birds multiply on the earth."
Reader 1:	Evening came, and morning followed—the fifth day.
Reader 2:	Then God said, "Let the earth bring forth all kinds of living creatures: cattle, creeping things, and wild animals of all kinds."

Reader 3:	And so it happened: God made all kinds of wild animals, all kinds of cattle, and all kinds of creeping things of the earth. God saw how good it was.
Reader 2:	Then God said, "Let us make man in our image, after our likeness. Let them have dominion over the fish of the sea, the birds of the air, and the cattle, and over all the wild animals and all the creatures that crawl on the ground."
Reader 3:	God created man in his image; in the divine image he created him; male and female he created them. God blessed them, saying:
Reader 2:	"Be fertile and multiply; fill the earth and subdue it. Have dominion over the fish of the sea, the birds of the air, and all the living things that move on the earth." God also said: "See, I give you every seed-bearing plant all over the earth and every tree that has seed-bearing fruit on it to be your food; and to all the animals of the land, all the birds of the air, and all the living creatures that crawl on the ground, I give all the green plants for food."
Reader 1:	And so it happened. God looked at everything he had made, and he found it very good. Evening came, and morning followed—the sixth day.
Reader 3:	Thus the heavens and the earth and all their array were completed. Since on the seventh day God was finished with the work he had been doing, he rested on the seventh day from all the work he had undertaken.
Reader 1:	This is the Word of the Lord.

Genesis 22:1-18

READING TWO

Reader 1: God put Abraham to the test. [He called to him, "Abraham!" "Ready!" he replied. Then] God said:

Reader 2: "Take your son Isaac, your only one, whom you love, and go to the land of Moriah. There you shall offer him up as a holocaust on a height that I will point out to you."

Reader 3: Early the next morning Abraham saddled his donkey, took with him his son Isaac, and two of his servants as well, and with the wood that he had cut for the holocaust, set out for the place of which God had told him.

Reader 1: On the third day Abraham got sight of the place from afar. Then he said to his servants:

Reader 3: "Both of you stay here with the donkey, while the boy and I go on over yonder. We will worship and then come back to you."

Reader 1: Thereupon Abraham took the wood for the holocaust and laid it on his son Isaac's shoulders, while he himself carried the fire and the knife. As the two walked on together, Isaac spoke to his father Abraham.

Reader 2: "Father!" [he said.]

Reader 3: "Yes, son," [he replied.]

Reader 2: [Isaac continued,] "Here are the fire and the wood, but where is the sheep for the holocaust?"

Reader 3:	"Son, [" Abraham answered, "] God himself will provide the sheep for the holocaust."
Reader 1:	Then the two continued going forward. When they came to the place of which God had told him, Abraham built an altar there and arranged the wood on it. Next he tied up his son Isaac and put him on top of the wood on the altar. Then he reached out and took the knife to slaughter his son. But the Lord's messenger called to him from heaven,
Reader 2:	"Abraham, Abraham!"
Reader 3:	"Yes, Lord," [he answered.]
Reader 2:	"Do not lay your hand on the boy, [" said the messenger."] Do not do the least thing to him. I know now how devoted you are to God, since you did not withhold from me your own beloved son."
Reader 1:	As Abraham looked about, he spied a ram caught by its horns in the thicket. So he went and took the ram and offered it up as a holocaust in place of his son.
Reader 3:	Abraham named the site Yahweh-yireh; hence people now say, "On the mountain the Lord will see." Again the Lord's messenger called to Abraham from heaven and said:
Reader 2:	"I swear by myself, [declares the Lord,] that because you acted as you did in not withholding from me your beloved son, I will bless you abundantly and make your descendants as countless as the stars of the sky and the sands of the seashore; your descendants shall take possession of the gates of their enemies, and in your descendants all the nations of the earth shall find blessing—all this because you obeyed my command."
Reader 1:	This is the Word of the Lord.

Exodus 14:15-15:1

READING THREE

Reader 1:   The Lord said to Moses,

Reader 2:   "Why are you crying out to me? Tell the Israelites to go forward. And you, lift up your staff and, with hand outstretched over the sea, split the sea in two, that the Israelites may pass through it on dry land. But I will make the Egyptians so obstinate that they will go in after them. Then I will receive glory through Pharaoh and all his army, his chariots and charioteers. The Egyptians shall know that I am the Lord, when I receive glory through Pharaoh and his chariots and charioteers."

Reader 3:   The angel of God, who had been leading Israel's camp, now moved and went around behind them. The column of cloud also, leaving the front, took up its place behind them so that it came between the camp of the Egyptians and that of Israel. But the cloud now became dark, and thus the night passed without the rival camps coming any closer together all night long.

Reader 1:   Then Moses stretched out his hand over the sea, and the Lord swept the sea with a strong east wind throughout the night and so turned it into dry land. When the water was thus divided, the Israelites marched into the midst of the sea on dry land, with the water like a wall to their right and to their left.

Reader 2:   The Egyptians followed in pursuit; all Pharaoh's horses and chariots and charioteers went after them right into the midst of the sea. In the night watch just before dawn the Lord cast through the column of the fiery cloud upon the Egyptian force a glance that threw it into a panic; and he so clogged their chariot wheels that they could hardly drive.

Reader 3: With that the Egyptians sounded the retreat before Israel, because the Lord was fighting for them against the Egyptians. Then the Lord told Moses,

Reader 2: "Stretch out your hand over the sea, that the water may flow back upon the Egyptians, upon their chariots and their charioteers."

Reader 1: So Moses stretched out his hand over the sea, and at dawn the sea flowed back to its normal depth. The Egyptians were fleeing head on toward the sea, when the Lord hurled them into its midst. As the water flowed back, it covered the chariots and the charioteers of Pharaoh's whole army which had followed the Israelites into the sea. Not a single one of them escaped.

Reader 3: But the Israelites had marched on dry land through the midst of the sea, with the water like a wall to their right and to their left. Thus the Lord saved Israel on that day from the power of the Egyptians.

Reader 2: When Israel saw the Egyptians lying dead on the seashore and beheld the great power that the Lord had shown against the Egyptians, they feared the Lord and believed in him and in his servant Moses.

Reader 1: Then Moses and the Israelites sang this song to the Lord:

All Readers: I will sing to the Lord, for he is gloriously triumphant; horse and chariot he has cast into the sea.

Reader 3: This is the Word of the Lord.

Years A, B, C/Lectionary no. 42-4

READING FOUR

Reader 1:   He who has become your husband is your Maker;
    his name is the Lord of hosts;
Your redeemer is the Holy One of Israel,
    called God of all the earth.

Reader 2:   The Lord calls you back,
    like a wife forsaken and grieved in spirit,
A wife married in youth and then cast off,
    says your God.

Reader 3:   For a brief moment I abandoned you,
    but with great tenderness I will take you back.
In an outburst of wrath, for a moment
    I hid my face from you;
But with enduring love I take pity on you,
    says the Lord, your redeemer.

Reader 2:   This is for me like the days of Noah,
    when I swore that the waters of Noah
    should never again deluge the earth;
So I have sworn not to be angry with you,
    or to rebuke you.

Reader 1:   Though the mountains leave their place
    and the hills be shaken,
My love shall never leave you
    nor my covenant of peace be shaken,
    says the Lord, who has mercy on you.

Reader 3:   O afflicted one, storm-battered and unconsoled,
    I lay your pavements in carnelians,
    and your foundations in sapphires:

Reader 1:   I will make your battlements of rubies,
                 your gates of carbuncles,
                 and all your walls of precious stones.

Reader 2:   All your sons shall be taught by the Lord,
                 and great shall be the peace of your children.
             In justice shall you be established,
                 far from the fear of oppression,
                 where destruction cannot come near you.

Reader 3:   This is the Word of the Lord.

Isaiah 55:1-11

READING FIVE

Reader 1:   Thus says the Lord:

Reader 2:   All you who are thirsty,
        come to the water!
    You who have no money,
        come, receive grain and eat;

Reader 3:   Come, without paying and without cost,
        drink wine and milk!
    Why spend your money for what is not bread;
        your wages for what fails to satisfy?

Reader 1:   Heed me, and you shall eat well,
        you shall delight in rich fare.
    Come to me heedfully,
        listen, that you may have life.

Reader 3:   I will renew with you the everlasting covenant,
        the benefits assured to David.

Reader 2:   As I made him a witness to the peoples,
        a leader and commander of nations,
    So shall you summon a nation you knew not,
        and nations that knew you not shall run to you,
    Because of the Lord, your God,
        the Holy One of Israel, who has glorified you.

Reader 1:   Seek the Lord while he may be found,
        call him while he is near.

Reader 2:   Let the scoundrel forsake his way,
        and the wicked man his thoughts;

Reader 3:	Let him turn to the Lord for mercy;
	to our God, who is generous in forgiving.

Reader 1: For my thoughts are not your thoughts,
    nor are your ways my ways, says the Lord.
As high as the heavens are above the earth,
    so high are my ways above your ways
    and my thoughts above your thoughts.

Reader 3: For just as from the heavens
    the rain and snow come down
And do not return there
    till they have watered the earth,
    making it fertile and fruitful,
Giving seed to him who sows
    and bread to him who eats,

Reader 2: So shall my words be
    that goes forth from my mouth;

Reader 3: It shall not return to me void,
    but shall do my will,
    achieving the end for which I sent it.

Reader 1: This is the Word of the Lord.

Baruch 3:9-15; 3:32-4:4

READING SIX

Reader 1:   Hear, O Israel, the commandments of life:
        listen, and know prudence!

Reader 2:   How is it, Israel,
        that you are in the land of your foes,
        grown old in a foreign land,
    Defiled with the dead,
        accounted with those destined for the nether world?

Reader 3:   You have forsaken the fountain of wisdom!

Reader 2:   Had you walked in the way of God,
        you would have dwelt in enduring peace.

Reader 3:   Learn where prudence is,
        where strength, where understanding;

Reader 1:   That you may know also
        where are length of days, and life,
        where light of the eyes, and peace.

Reader 3:   Who has found the place of wisdom,
        who has entered into her treasuries?

Reader 2:   He who knows all things knows her;

Reader 1:   he has probed her by his knowledge—
    He who established the earth for all time,
        and filled it with four-footed beasts;

Reader 2:   He who dismisses the light, and it departs,
        calls it, and it obeys him trembling;

Reader 3: Before whom the stars at their posts
    shine and rejoice;
When he calls them, they answer, "Here we are!"
    shining with joy for their Maker.

Reader 2: Such is our God;

Reader 3:   no other is to be compared to him:

Reader 1: He has traced out all the way of understanding,
    and has given her to Jacob, his servant,
    to Israel, his beloved son.

Reader 3: Since then she has appeared on earth,
    and moved among men.
She is the book of the precepts of God,
    the law that endures forever;

Reader 2: All who cling to her will live,
    but those will die who forsake her.

Reader 1: Turn, O Jacob, and receive her:
    walk by her light toward splendor.

Reader 3: Give not your glory to another,
    your privileges to an alien race.

Reader 1: Blessed are we, O Israel;
    for what pleases God is known to us!

Reader 2: This is the Word of the Lord.

Years A, B, C/Lectionary no. 42-7

Ezekiel 36:16-28

READING SEVEN

Reader 1:   Thus the word of the Lord came to me:

Reader 2:   Son of man, when the house of Israel lived in their land, they defiled it by their conduct and deeds. In my sight their conduct was like the defilement of a menstruous woman. Therefore I poured out my fury upon them because of the blood which they poured out on the ground, and because they defiled it with idols.

Reader 3:   I scattered them among the nations, dispersing them over foreign lands; according to their conduct and deeds I judged them.

Reader 1:   But when they came among the nations wherever they came, they served to profane my holy name, because it was said of them: "These are the people of the Lord, yet they had to leave their land."

Reader 3:   So I have relented because of my holy name which the house of Israel profaned among the nations where they came.

Reader 2:   Therefore say to the house of Israel: Thus says the Lord God: Not for your sakes do I act, house of Israel, but for the sake of my holy name, which you profaned among the nations to which you came.

Reader 1:   I will prove the holiness of my great name, profaned among the nations, in whose midst you have profaned it. Thus the nations shall know that I am the Lord, says the Lord God, when in their sight I prove my holiness through you.

Reader 2:   For I will take you away from among the nations, gather you from all the foreign lands, and bring you back to your own land.

Reader 1:   I will sprinkle clean water upon you to cleanse you from all your impurities, and from all your idols I will cleanse you.

Reader 3:   I will give you a new heart and place a new spirit within you, taking from your bodies your stony hearts and giving you natural hearts.

Reader 1:   I will put my spirit within you and make you live by my statutes, careful to observe my decrees.

Reader 3:   You shall live in the land I gave your fathers;

Reader 2:   you shall be my people, and I will be your God.

Reader 1:   This is the Word of the Lord.

Romans 6:3-11

EPISTLE

Reader 1: Are you not aware that we who were baptized into Christ Jesus were baptized into his death?

Reader 3: Through baptism into his death we were buried with him, so that, just as Christ was raised from the dead by the glory of the Father, we too might live a new life.

Reader 2: If we have been united with him through likeness to his death, so shall we be through a like resurrection.

Reader 1: This we know: our old self was crucified with him so that the sinful body might be destroyed and we might be slaves to sin no longer.

Reader 2: A man who is dead has been freed from sin.

Reader 3: If we have died with Christ, we believe that we are also to live with him.

Reader 2: We know that Christ, once raised from the dead, will never die again; death has no more power over him.

Reader 1: His death was death to sin, once for all;

Reader 3: his life is life for God.

Reader 1: In the same way, you must consider yourselves dead to sin but alive for God in Christ Jesus.

Reader 2: This is the Word of the Lord

Years A, B, C/Lectionary no. 42

A: Matthew 28:1-10
B: Mark 16:1-8
C: Luke 24:1-12

[Year A]

Gospel Reading

Reader 1: After the sabbath, as the first day of the week was dawning, Mary Magdalene came with the other Mary to inspect the tomb.

Reader 2: Suddenly there was a mighty earthquake, as the angel of the Lord descended from heaven. He came to the stone, rolled it back, and sat on it. In appearance he resembled a flash of lightning while his garments were as dazzling as snow.

Reader 3: The guards grew paralyzed with fear of him and fell down like dead men. Then the angel spoke, addressing the women:

Reader 1: "Do not be frightened. I know you are looking for Jesus the crucified, but he is not here. He has been raised, exactly as he promised. Come and see the spot where he was laid. Then go quickly and tell his disciples: 'He has been raised from the dead and now goes ahead of you to Galilee, where you will see him.' That is the message I have for you."

Reader 3: They hurried away from the tomb half-overjoyed, half-fearful, and ran to carry the good news to his disciples.

Reader 2: Suddenly, without warning, Jesus stood before them and said, "Peace!" The women came up and embraced his feet and did him homage. At this Jesus said to them,

Reader 3: "Do not be afraid! Go and carry the news to my brothers that they are to go to Galilee, where they will see me."

Reader 1: This is the gospel of the Lord.

Reader 1: When the sabbath was over, Mary Magdalene, Mary the mother of James, and Salome bought perfumed oils with which they intended to go and anoint Jesus.

Reader 2: Very early, just after sunrise, on the first day of the week they came to the tomb. They were saying to one another,

Reader 3: "Who will roll back the stone for us from the entrance to the tomb?"

Reader 2: When they looked, they found that the stone had been rolled back. (It was a huge one.) On entering the tomb they saw a young man sitting at the right, dressed in a white robe. This frightened them thoroughly, but he reassured them:

Reader 1: "You need not be amazed! You are looking for Jesus of Nazareth, the one who was crucified. He has been raised up; he is not here. See the place where they laid him. Go now and tell his disciples and Peter, 'He is going ahead of you to Galilee, where you will see him just as he told you.' "

Reader 3: They made their way out and fled from the tomb bewildered and trembling; and because of their great fear, they said nothing to anyone.

Reader 2: This is the gospel of the Lord.

Reader 1: On the first day of the week, at dawn, the women came to the tomb bringing the spices they had prepared. They found the stone rolled back from the tomb; but when they entered the tomb, they did not find the body of the Lord Jesus.

Reader 2: While they were still at a loss what to think of this, two men in dazzling garments appeared beside them. Terrified, the women bowed to the ground. The men said to them:

Reader 3: "Why do you search among the dead for the living One? He is not here; he has been raised up. Remember what he said to you while he was still in Galilee—that the Son of Man must be delivered into the hands of sinful men, and be crucified, and on the third day rise again."

Reader 2: With this reminder, his words came back to them. On their return from the tomb, they told all these things to the Eleven and the others.

Reader 1: The women were Mary of Magdala, Joanna, and Mary the mother of James. The other women with them also told the apostles, but the story seemed like nonsense and they refused to believe them.

Reader 3: Peter, however, got up and ran to the tomb. He stooped down but could see nothing but the wrappings. So he went away full of amazement at what had occurred.

Reader 2: This is the gospel of the Lord.

Easter Sunday

(The three readings are interwoven into one continuous reading.)

Years A, B, C/Lectionary no. 43

John 20:1-9
Acts 10:34,37-43
Colossians 3:1-4 (or)
1 Corinthians 5:6-8

Reader 1: Early in the morning on the first day of the week, while it was still dark, Mary Magdalene came to the tomb. She saw that the stone had been moved away, so she ran off to Simon Peter and the other disciple (the one Jesus loved) and told them,

Reader 2: "The Lord has been taken from the tomb! We don't know where they have put him!"

Reader 3: At that, Peter and the other disciple started out on their way toward the tomb. They were running side by side, but then the other disciple outran Peter and reached the tomb first. He did not enter but bent down to peer in, and saw the wrappings lying on the ground.

Reader 2: Presently, Simon Peter came along behind him and entered the tomb. He observed the wrappings on the ground and saw the piece of cloth which had covered the head not lying with the wrappings, but rolled up in a place by itself.

Reader 3: Then the disciple who had arrived first at the tomb went in. He saw and believed. (Remember, as yet they did not understand the Scripture that Jesus had to rise from the dead.)

Reader 1: *Much later, after understanding had come,* Peter addressed the people in these words: "I take it you know what has been reported all over Judea about Jesus of Nazareth, beginning in Galilee with the baptism John preached; of the way God anointed him with the Holy Spirit and power.

Reader 3: "He went about doing good works and healing all who were in the grip of the devil, and God was with him. We are witnesses to all that he did in the land of the Jews and in Jerusalem.

Reader 2: "They killed him finally, 'hanging him on a tree,' only to have God raise him up on the third day and grant that he be seen, not by all, but only by such witnesses as had been chosen beforehand by God—by us who ate and drank with him after he rose from the dead.

Reader 1: "He commissioned us to preach to the people and to bear witness that he is the one set apart by God as judge of the living and the dead. To him all the prophets testify, saying that everyone who believes in him has forgiveness of sins through his name."

Reader 2: *And that is why the Apostle Paul advises us:*

Since you have been raised up in company with Christ, set your heart on what pertains to higher realms where Christ is seated at God's right hand. Be intent on things above rather than on things of earth.	or	Do you not know that a little yeast has its effects all through the dough? Get rid of the old yeast to make of yourselves fresh dough, unleavened loaves, as it were;

Reader 3:

After all, you have died! Your life is hidden now with Christ in God. When Christ our life appears, then you shall appear with him in glory.	or	Christ our Passover has been sacrificed. Let us celebrate the feast not with the old yeast, that of corruption and wickedness, but with the unleavened bread of sincerity and truth.

Reader 1: This is the Word of the Lord.

Second Sunday of Easter

Years A, B, C/Lectionary nos. 44-45-46

John 20:19-31

Narrator:	On the evening of that first day of the week, even though the disciples had locked the doors of the place where they were for fear of the Jews, Jesus came and stood before them.
Jesus:	"Peace be with you," [he said.]
Narrator:	When he had said this, he showed them his hands and his side. At the sight of the Lord, the disciples rejoiced.
Jesus:	"Peace be with you, [" he said again.] As the Father has sent me, so I send you."
Narrator:	Then he breathed on them and said:
Jesus:	"Receive the Holy Spirit. If you forgive men's sins, they are forgiven them; if you hold them bound, they are held bound."
Narrator:	It happened that one of the Twelve, Thomas (the name means "Twin"), was absent when Jesus came. The other disciples kept telling him: "We have seen the Lord!" His answer was,
Thomas:	"I'll never believe it without probing the nail-prints in his hands, without putting my finger in the nail-marks and my hand into his side."
Narrator:	A week later, the disciples were once more in the room, and this time Thomas was with them. Despite the locked doors, Jesus came and stood before them.

Jesus:	"Peace be with you," [he said;]
Narrator:	then, to Thomas:
Jesus:	"Take your finger and examine my hands. Put your hand into my side. Do not persist in your unbelief, but believe!"
Thomas:	[Thomas said in response,] "My Lord and my God!"
Jesus:	[Jesus then said to him:]
	"You became a believer because you saw me. Blest are they who have not seen and have believed."
Narrator:	Jesus performed many other signs as well—signs not recorded here—in the presence of his disciples. But these have been recorded to help you believe that Jesus is the Messiah, the Son of God, so that through this faith you may have life in his name.
	This is the gospel of the Lord.

Third Sunday of Easter

(Years A and B are combined in one reading.)

Years A, B/Lectionary nos. 47, 48

Luke 24:13-35
Luke 24:35-48

Narrator: Two disciples of Jesus that same day, the first day of the week, were making their way to a village named Emmaus, seven miles distant from Jerusalem, discussing as they went all that had happened. In the course of their lively exchange, Jesus approached and began to walk along with them. However, they were restrained from recognizing him. He said to them,

Jesus: "What are you discussing as you go your way?"

Narrator: They halted in distress, and one of them, Cleopas by name, asked him,

Speaker: "Are you the only resident of Jerusalem who does not know the things that went on there these past few days?"

Jesus: [He said to them,] "What things?"

Speaker: [They said:] "All those that had to do with Jesus of Nazareth, a prophet powerful in word and deed in the eyes of God and all the people; how our chief priests and leaders delivered him up to be condemned to death, and crucified him. We were hoping that he was the one who would set Israel free. Besides all this, today, the third day since these things happened, some women of our group have just brought us some astonishing news. They were at the tomb before dawn and failed to find his body, but returned with the tale that they had seen a vision of angels who declared he was alive. Some of our number went to the tomb and found it to be just as the women said; but him they did not see."

Jesus:	[Then he said to them,] "What little sense you have! How slow you are to believe all that the prophets have announced! Did not the Messiah have to undergo all this so as to enter into his glory?"
Narrator:	Beginning, then, with Moses and all the prophets, he interpreted for them every passage of Scripture which referred to him. By now they were near the village to which they were going, and he acted as if he were going farther. But they pressed him:
Speaker:	"Stay with us. It is nearly evening—the day is practically over."
Narrator:	So he went in to stay with them. When he had seated himself with them to eat, he took bread, pronounced the blessing, then broke the bread and began to distribute it to them. With that their eyes were opened and they recognized him; whereupon he vanished from their sight. They said to one another,
Speaker:	"Were not our hearts burning inside us as he talked to us on the road and explained the Scriptures to us?"
Narrator:	They got up immediately and returned to Jerusalem, where they found the Eleven and the rest of the company assembled. They were greeted with,
Speaker:	"The Lord has been raised! It is true! He has appeared to Simon."
Narrator:	Then they recounted what had happened on the road and how they had come to know him in the breaking of the bread. While they were still speaking about all this, he himself stood in their midst and said to them,
Jesus:	"Peace to you."
Narrator:	In their panic and fright they thought they were seeing a ghost. He said to them,

Jesus:	"Why are you disturbed? Why do such ideas cross your mind? Look at my hands and my feet; it is really I. Touch me, and see that a ghost does not have flesh and bones as I do."
Narrator:	As he said this he showed them his hands and feet. They were still incredulous for sheer joy and wonder, so he said to them,
Jesus:	"Have you anything here to eat?"
Narrator:	They gave him a piece of cooked fish, which he took and ate in their presence. Then he said to them,
Jesus:	"Recall those words I spoke to you when I was still with you: everything in the law of Moses and the prophets and psalms had to be fulfilled."
Narrator:	Then he opened their minds to the understanding of the Scriptures. He said to them:
Jesus:	"Thus it is likewise written that the Messiah must suffer and rise from the dead on the third day. In his name, penance for the remission of sins is to be preached to all the nations, beginning at Jerusalem. You are witnesses of this."
Narrator:	This is the gospel of the Lord.

Third Sunday of Easter

Year C/Lectionary no. 49

John 21:1-19

Narrator:	At the Sea of Tiberias Jesus showed himself to the disciples once again. This is how the appearance took place. Assembled were Simon Peter, Thomas ("the Twin"), Nathanael (from Cana in Galilee), Zebedee's sons, and two other disciples. Simon Peter said to them,
Speaker:	"I'm going out to fish."
Narrator:	"We'll join you," they replied, and went off to get into their boat. All through the night they caught nothing. Just after daybreak Jesus was standing on the shore, though none of the disciples knew it was Jesus. He said to them,
Jesus:	"Children, have you caught anything to eat?"
Speaker:	"Not a thing," [they answered.]
Jesus:	"Cast your net off to the starboard side, [" he suggested, "] and you will find something."
Narrator:	So they made a cast, and took so many fish they could not haul the net in. Then the disciple Jesus loved cried out to Peter,
Speaker:	"It is the Lord!"
Narrator:	On hearing it was the Lord, Simon Peter threw on some clothes—he was stripped—and jumped into the water. Meanwhile the other disciples came in the boat, towing the net full of fish. Actually they were not far from land—no more than a hundred yards. When they landed, they saw a charcoal fire there with a fish laid on it and some bread.
Jesus:	"Bring some of the fish you just caught," [Jesus told them.]

Narrator:	Simon Peter went aboard and hauled ashore the net loaded with sizable fish—one hundred fifty-three of them! In spite of the great number, the net was not torn.
Jesus:	"Come and eat your meal," [Jesus told them.]
Narrator:	Not one of the disciples presumed to inquire, "Who are you?" for they knew it was the Lord. Jesus came over, took the bread and gave it to them, and did the same with the fish. This marked the third time that Jesus appeared to the disciples after being raised from the dead. When they had eaten their meal, Jesus said to Simon Peter,
Jesus:	"Simon, son of John, do you love me more than these?"
Speaker:	"Yes, Lord, [" Peter said, "] you know that I love you."
Jesus:	[At which Jesus said,] "Feed my lambs."
Narrator:	A second time he put his question,
Jesus:	"Simon, son of John, do you love me?"
Speaker:	"Yes, Lord, [" Peter said, "] you know that I love you."
Jesus:	[Jesus replied,] "Tend my sheep."
Narrator:	A third time Jesus asked him,
Jesus:	"Simon, son of John, do you love me?"
Narrator:	Peter was hurt because he had asked a third time, "Do you love me?" So he said to him:
Speaker:	"Lord, you know everything. You know well that I love you."
Jesus:	[Jesus told him,] "Feed my sheep.

"I tell you solemnly:
as a young man
you fastened your belt

and went about as you pleased;
but when you are older
you will stretch out your hands,
and another will tie you fast
and carry you off against your will.''

Narrator: (What he said indicated the sort of death by which Peter was to glorify God.) When Jesus had finished speaking he said to him,

Jesus: ''Follow me.''

Narrator: This is the gospel of the Lord.

Fourth Sunday of Easter

Year A/Lectionary no. 50

Acts 2:14,36-41
1 Peter 2:20-25

ACTS Reading

Narrator: On the day of Pentecost Peter stood up with the Eleven, raised his voice, and addressed them:

Peter: "Let the whole house of Israel know beyond any doubt that God has made both Lord and Messiah this Jesus whom you crucified."

Narrator: When they heard this, they were deeply shaken. They asked Peter and the other apostles,

Speaker: "What are we to do, brothers?"

Peter: [Peter answered:] "You must reform and be baptized, each one of you, in the name of Jesus Christ, that your sins may be forgiven; then you will receive the gift of the Holy Spirit. It was to you and your children that the promise was made, and to all those still far off whom the Lord our God calls."

Narrator: In support of his testimony he used many other arguments, and kept urging,

Peter: "Save yourselves from this generation which has gone astray."

Speaker: Those who accepted his message were baptized; some three thousand were added that day.

Narrator: This is the Word of the Lord.

1 PETER Reading

Reader 1:   If you put up with suffering for doing what is right, this is acceptable in God's eyes.

Reader 2:   It was for this you were called, since Christ suffered for you in just this way and left you an example, to have you follow in his footsteps.

Reader 3:   He did no wrong; no deceit was found in his mouth.

Reader 1:   When he was insulted he returned no insult.

Reader 3:   When he was made to suffer, he did not counter with threats.

Reader 2:   Instead, he delivered himself up to the One who judges justly.

Reader 1:   In his own body he brought your sins to the cross, so that all of us, dead to sin, could live in accord with God's will.

Reader 2:   By his wounds you were healed.

Reader 3:   At one time you were straying like sheep, but now you have returned to the shepherd, the guardian of your souls.

Reader 1:   This is the Word of the Lord.

Sixth Sunday of Easter

Year B/Lectionary no. 57

Acts 10:25-26,34-35,44-48

Reader 1: Peter entered the house of Cornelius who met him, dropped to his knees before Peter and bowed low. Peter said as he helped him to his feet,

Peter: "Get up! I am only a man myself."

Reader 2: Peter proceeded to address the relatives and friends of Cornelius in these words:

Peter: "I begin to see how true it is that God shows no partiality. Rather, the man of any nation who fears God and acts uprightly is acceptable to him."

Reader 1: Peter had not finished these words when the Holy Spirit descended upon all who were listening to Peter's message.

Reader 2: The circumcised believers who had accompanied Peter were surprised that the gift of the Holy Spirit should have been poured out on the Gentiles also, whom they could hear speaking in tongues and glorifying God.

Reader 1: Peter put the question at that point:

Peter: "What can stop these people who have received the Holy Spirit, even as we have, from being baptized with water?"

Reader 2: So he gave orders that they be baptized in the name of Jesus Christ. After this was done, they asked him to stay with them for a few days.

This is the Word of the Lord.

Ascension

Acts 1:1-11
A: Matthew 28:16-20
B: Mark 16:15-20
C: Luke 24:46-53
Ephesians 1:17-23

ACTS Reading

Reader 1: In my first account, Theophilus, I dealt with all that Jesus did and taught until the day he was taken up to heaven, having first instructed the apostles he had chosen through the Holy Spirit. In the time after his suffering he showed them in many convincing ways that he was alive, appearing to them over the course of forty days and speaking to them about the reign of God. On one occasion when he met with them, he told them not to leave Jerusalem:

Reader 2: "Wait, rather, for the fulfillment of my Father's promise, of which you have heard me speak. John baptized with water, but within a few days you will be baptized with the Holy Spirit."

Reader 1: While they were with him they asked,

Reader 3: "Lord, are you going to restore the rule to Israel now?"

Reader 2: [His answer was:] "The exact time is not yours to know. The Father has reserved that to himself. You will receive power when the Holy Spirit comes down on you; then you are to be my witnesses in Jerusalem, throughout Judea and Samaria, yes, even to the ends of the earth."

[Year A]

MATTHEW Reading

Reader 1: The eleven disciples made their way to Galilee, to the mountain to which Jesus had summoned them. At the sight of him, those who had entertained doubts fell down in

119

homage. Jesus came forward and addressed them in these words:

Reader 2:

"Full authority has been given to me
both in heaven and on earth;
go, therefore, and make disciples of all the nations.
Baptize them in the name
    'of the Father,
    and of the Son,
    and of the Holy Spirit.'
Teach them to carry out everything I have commanded
    you.
And know that I am with you always, until the
    end of the world!''

[Year B]

MARK Reading

Reader 1:   Jesus appeared to the Eleven, and said to them:

Reader 2:   "Go into the whole world and proclaim the good news to all creation. The man who believes in it and accepts baptism will be saved; the man who refuses to believe in it will be condemned. Signs like these will accompany those who have professed their faith: they will use my name to expel demons, they will speak entirely new languages, they will be able to handle serpents, they will be able to drink deadly poison without harm, and the sick upon whom they will lay their hands will recover.''

Reader 3:   Then, after speaking to them, the Lord Jesus was taken up into heaven and took his seat at God's right hand. The Eleven went forth and preached everywhere. The Lord continued to work with them throughout and confirm the message through the signs which accompanied them.

[Year C]

LUKE Reading

Reader 2:   [Jesus said to the Eleven: "Thus] it is written that the

120

Messiah must suffer and rise from the dead on the third day. In his name, penance for the remission of sins is to be preached to the nations, beginning at Jerusalem. You are witnesses of all this. See, I send down upon you the promise of my Father. Remain here in the city until you are clothed with power from on high.''

Reader 3:   He then led them out near Bethany, and with hands upraised, blessed them. As he blessed, he left them, and was taken up to heaven. They fell down to do him reverence, then returned to Jerusalem filled with joy. There they were to be found in the temple constantly, speaking the praises of God.

[All Years]

EPHESIANS Reading

Reader 1:   *And so* may the God of our Lord Jesus Christ, the Father of glory, grant you a spirit of wisdom and insight to know him clearly.

Reader 2:   May he enlighten your innermost vision that you may know the great hope to which he has called you, the wealth of his glorious heritage to be distributed among the members of the church, and the immeasurable scope of his power in us who believe.

Reader 1:   It is like the strength he showed in raising Christ from the dead and seating him at his right hand in heaven, high above every principality, power, virtue and domination, and every name that can be given in this age or the age to come.

Reader 3:   He has put all things under Christ's feet and has made him thus exalted, head of the church, which is his body: the fullness of him who fills the universe in all its parts.

This is the Word of the Lord.

Pentecost Sunday

(The three readings for Pentecost are interwoven into one continuous reading.)

Years A, B, C/Lectionary no. 64

John 20:19-23
Acts 2:1-11
1 Corinthians 12:3-7,12-13

Narrator: On the evening of that first day of the week, even though the disciples had locked the doors of the place where they were for fear of the Jews, Jesus came and stood before them.

Reader 1:   "Peace be with you," [he said.]

Narrator: When he had said this, he showed them his hands and his side. At the sight of the Lord the disciples rejoiced.

Reader 1:   "Peace be with you, [" he said again.]

"As the Father has sent me,
so I send you."

Narrator: Then he breathed on them and said:

Reader 1:   "Receive the Holy Spirit.
If you forgive men's sins,
they are forgiven them;
if you hold them bound,
they are held bound."

Reader 2:   When the day of Pentecost came it found them gathered in one place. Suddenly from up in the sky there came a noise like a strong, driving wind which was heard all through the house where they were seated. Tongues as of fire appeared which parted and came to rest on each of them.

Narrator: All were filled with the Holy Spirit.

122

Reader 1:   They began to express themselves in foreign tongues and make bold proclamations as the Spirit prompted them.

Narrator: No one can say: "Jesus is Lord," except in the Holy Spirit. There are different gifts but the same Spirit; there are different ministries but the same Lord; there are different works but the same God who accomplishes all of them in everyone.

Reader 2:   To each person the manifestation of the Spirit is given for the common good. The body is one and has many members, but all the members, many though they are, are one body;

Reader 1:   and so it is with Christ. It was in one Spirit that all of us, whether Jew or Greek, slave or free, were baptized into one body. All of us have been given to drink of the one Spirit.

Narrator: Staying in Jerusalem at the time were devout Jews of every nation under heaven. These heard the sound, and assembled in a large crowd. They were much confused because each one heard these men speaking his own language. The whole occurrence astonished them. They asked in utter amazement,

Reader 2:   "Are not all of these men who are speaking Galileans? How is it that each of us hears them in his native tongue?

Reader 1:   "We are Parthians, Medes, and Elamites.

Narrator: "We live in Mesopotamia, Judea and Cappadocia, Pontus, the province of Asia, Phrygia and Pamphylia, Egypt, and the regions of Libya around Cyrene.

Reader 2:   "There are even visitors from Rome—all Jews, or those who have come over to Judaism; Cretans and Arabs too.

Narrator: "Yet each of us hears them speaking in his own tongue about the marvels God has accomplished."

This is the Word of the Lord.

ORDINARY TIME

Second Sunday in Ordinary Time

Year B/Lectionary no. 66

1 Samuel 3:3-10,19

Narrator:	Samuel was sleeping in the temple of the Lord where the ark of God was. The Lord called to Samuel, who answered,
Samuel:	"Here I am."
Narrator:	He ran to Eli and said,
Samuel:	"Here I am. You called me."
Eli:	"I did not call you, [" Eli said. "] Go back to sleep."
Narrator:	So he went back to sleep. Again the Lord called Samuel, who rose and went to Eli.
Samuel:	"Here I am, [" he said. "] You called me."
Eli:	[But he answered,] "I did not call you, my son. Go back to sleep."
Narrator:	At that time Samuel was not familiar with the Lord, because the Lord had not revealed anything to him as yet. The Lord called Samuel again, for the third time. Getting up and going to Eli, he said,
Samuel:	"Here I am. You called me."
Narrator:	Then Eli understood that the Lord was calling the youth. So he said to Samuel,
Eli:	"Go to sleep, and if you are called, reply, 'Speak, Lord, for your servant is listening.' "
Narrator:	When Samuel went to sleep in his place, the Lord came and revealed his presence, calling out as before, "Samuel, Samuel!" Samuel answered,

Samuel:	"Speak, Lord, for your servant is listening."
Narrator:	Samuel grew up, and the Lord was with him, not permitting any word of his to be without effect.
	This is the Word of the Lord.

Second Sunday in Ordinary Time

Year C/Lectionary no. 67

John 2:1-12

Narrator: There was a wedding at Cana in Galilee, and the mother of Jesus was there. Jesus and his disciples had likewise been invited to the celebration. At a certain point the wine ran out, and Jesus' mother told him,

Speaker: "They have no more wine."

Jesus: [Jesus replied,] "Woman, how does this concern of yours involve me? My hour has not yet come."

Narrator: His mother instructed those waiting on table,

Speaker: "Do whatever he tells you."

Narrator: As prescribed for Jewish ceremonial washings, there were at hand six stone water jars, each one holding fifteen to twenty-five gallons.

Jesus: "Fill those jars with water," [Jesus ordered.]

Narrator: at which they filled them to the brim.

Jesus: "Now, [" he said, "] draw some out and take it to the waiter in charge."

Narrator: They did as he instructed them. The waiter in charge tasted the water made wine, without knowing where it had come from; only the waiters knew, since they had drawn the water. Then the waiter in charge called the groom over and remarked to him:

Speaker: "People usually serve the choice wine first; then when the guests have been drinking awhile, a lesser vintage. What you have done is keep the choice wine until now."

Narrator: Jesus performed this first of his signs at Cana in Galilee. Thus did he reveal his glory, and his disciples believed in him. After this he went down to Capernaum, along with his mother and brothers and his disciples but they stayed there only a few days.

This is the gospel of the Lord.

Fourth Sunday in Ordinary Time

Year A/Lectionary no. 71

Matthew 5:1-12

Reader 1:   When Jesus saw the crowds, he went up on the mountainside. After he had sat down his disciples gathered around him, and he began to teach them:

Reader 2:   "How blest are the poor in spirit: the reign of God is theirs.

Reader 3:   "Blest too are the sorrowing; they shall be consoled.

Reader 2:   "Blest are the lowly; they shall inherit the land.

Reader 1:   "Blest are they who hunger and thirst for holiness; they shall have their fill.

Reader 3:   "Blest are they who show mercy; mercy shall be theirs.

Reader 1:   "Blest are the single-hearted, for they shall see God.

Reader 3:   "Blest too the peacemakers; they shall be called sons of God.

Reader 2:   "Blest are those persecuted for holiness' sake; the reign of God is theirs.

Reader 1:   "Blest are you when they insult you and persecute you and utter every kind of slander against you because of me.

Reader 2:   "Be glad and rejoice, for your reward in heaven is great."

Reader 3:   This is the gospel of the Lord.

Sixth Sunday in Ordinary Time

Year C/Lectionary no. 79

Luke 6:17,20-26

Reader 1: When Jesus came down the mountain, he stopped at a level stretch where there were many of his disciples;

Reader 2: a large crowd of people was with them from all Judea and Jerusalem and the coast of Tyre and Sidon.

Reader 3: Then, raising his eyes to his disciples, he said:

Reader 1: "Blest are you poor;

Reader 3: "the reign of God is yours.

Reader 1: "Blest are you who hunger;

Reader 2: "filled you shall be.

Reader 1: "Blest are you who are weeping;

Reader 3: "you shall laugh.

Reader 1: "Blest shall you be when men hate you, when they ostrasize you and insult you and proscribe your name as evil because of the Son of Man.

Reader 2: "On the day they do so, rejoice and exult, for your reward shall be great in heaven. Thus it was that their fathers treated the prophets.

Reader 3: "But woe to you rich,

Reader 1: "for your consolation is now.

Reader 3: "Woe to you who are full;

Reader 2: "you shall go hungry.

Reader 3:   "Woe to you who laugh now;

Reader 1:   "you shall weep in your grief.

Reader 3:   "Woe to you when all speak well of you.

Reader 2:   "Their fathers treated the false prophets in just this way."

Reader 1:   This is the gospel of the Lord.

Tenth Sunday in Ordinary Time

Year B/Lectionary no. 90

Genesis 3:9-15
Mark 3:20-35

GENESIS Reading

Narrator: After Adam had eaten of the tree the Lord God called him and asked him,

God: "Where are you?"

Speaker: [He answered,] "I heard you in the garden; but I was afraid, because I was naked, so I hid myself."

God: [Then he asked,] "Who told you that you were naked? You have eaten, then, from the tree of which I had forbidden you to eat!"

Speaker: [The man replied,] "The woman whom you put here with me—she gave me fruit from the tree, and so I ate it."

Narrator: The Lord God then asked the woman,

God: "Why did you do such a thing?"

Narrator: The woman answered,

Speaker: "The serpent tricked me into it, so I ate it."

Narrator: Then the Lord God said to the serpent:

God: "Because you have done this, you shall be banned
from all the animals
and from all the wild creatures.
On your belly shall you crawl,
and dirt shall you eat
all the days of your life.

I will put enmity between you and the woman,
　　and between your offspring and hers;
He will strike at your head,
　　while you strike at his heel.''

Narrator:　　This is the Word of the Lord.

MARK Reading

Narrator:　　Jesus came to the house with his disciples and again the crowd assembled, making it impossible for them to get any food whatever. When his family heard of this they came to take charge of him, saying,

Speaker:　　"He is out of his mind";

Narrator:　　while the scribes who arrived from Jerusalem asserted,

Speaker:　　"He is possessed by Beelzebul, ['' and ''] He expels demons with the help of the prince of demons.''

Narrator:　　Summoning them, he then began to speak to them by way of examples:

Jesus:　　"How can Satan expel Satan? If a kingdom is torn by civil strife, that kingdom cannot last. If a household is divided according to loyalties, that household will not survive. Similarly, if Satan has suffered mutiny in his ranks and is torn by dissension, he cannot endure; he is finished. No one can enter a strong man's house and despoil his property unless he has first put him under restraint. Only then can he plunder his house. I give you my word, every sin will be forgiven mankind and all the blasphemies men utter, but whoever blasphemes against the Holy Spirit will never be forgiven. He carries the guilt of his sin without end.''

Narrator:　　He spoke thus because they had said, "He is possessed by an unclean spirit.'' His mother and his brothers arrived, and as they stood outside they sent word to him to come out. The crowd seated around him told him,

Speaker:	"Your mother and your brothers and your sisters are outside asking for you."
Narrator:	He said in reply,
Jesus:	"Who are my mother and my brothers?"
Narrator:	And gazing around him at those seated in the circle he continued,
Jesus:	"These are my mother and my brothers. Whoever does the will of God is brother and sister and mother to me."
Narrator	This is the gospel of the Lord.

Tenth Sunday in Ordinary Time

Year C/Lectionary no. 91

1 Kings 17:17-24

Narrator: The son of the mistress of the house fell sick, and his sickness grew more severe until he stopped breathing. So she said to Elijah,

Woman: "Why have you done this to me, O man of God? Have you come to me to call attention to my guilt and to kill my son?"

Elijah: "Give me your son," [Elijah said to her.]

Narrator: Taking him from her lap, he carried him to the upper room where he was staying, and laid him on his own bed. He called out to the Lord:

Elijah: "O Lord, my God, will you afflict even the widow with whom I am staying by killing her son?"

Narrator: Then he stretched himself out upon the child three times and called out to the Lord:

Elijah: "O Lord, my God, let the life breath return to the body of this child."

Narrator: The Lord heard the prayer of Elijah; the life breath returned to the child's body and he revived. Taking the child, Elijah brought him down into the house from the upper room and gave him to his mother.

Elijah: "See! [" Elijah said to her,"] your son is alive."

Woman: "Now indeed I know that you are a man of God, [" the woman replied to Elijah."] The word of the Lord comes truly from your mouth."

Narrator: This is the Word of the Lord.

Eleventh Sunday in Ordinary Time

Year C/Lectionary no. 94

Luke 7:36-8:3

Narrator:	There was a certain Pharisee who invited Jesus to dine with him. Jesus went to the Pharisee's home and reclined to eat. A woman known in the town to be a sinner learned that he was dining in the Pharisee's home. She brought in a vase of perfumed oil and stood behind him at his feet, weeping so that her tears fell upon his feet. Then she wiped them with her hair, kissing them and perfuming them with the oil. When his host, the Pharisee, saw this, he said to himself,
Speaker:	"If this man were a prophet, he would know who and what sort of woman this is that touches him—that she is a sinner."
Narrator:	In answer to his thoughts, Jesus said to him,
Jesus:	"Simon, I have something to propose to you."
Speaker:	"Teacher, speak."
Jesus:	"Two men owed money to a certain money-lender; one owed a total of five hundred coins, the other fifty. Since neither was able to repay, he wrote off both debts. Which of them was more grateful to him?"
Speaker:	"He, I presume, to whom he remitted the larger sum."
Jesus:	"You are right."
Narrator:	Turning then to the woman, Jesus said to Simon:
Jesus:	"You see this woman? I came to your home and you provided me with no water for my feet. She has washed my feet with her tears and wiped them with her hair. You gave me no kiss, but she has not ceased kissing my feet since I

entered. You did not anoint my head with oil, but she has anointed my feet with perfume. I tell you, that is why her many sins are forgiven—because of her great love. Little is forgiven the one whose love is small.''

Narrator: He said to the woman then,

Jesus: "Your sins are forgiven,"

Narrator: at which his fellow guests began to ask among themselves,

Speaker: "Who is this that he even forgives sins?"

Narrator: Meanwhile Jesus said to the woman,

Jesus: "Your faith has been your salvation. Go now in peace."

Narrator: After this he journeyed through towns and villages preaching and proclaiming the good news of the kingdom of God. The Twelve accompanied him, and also some women who had been cured of evil spirits and maladies: Mary called the Magdalene, from whom seven devils had gone out, Joanna, the wife of Herod's steward Chuza, Susanna, and many others who were assisting them out of their means.

This is the gospel of the Lord.

Thirteenth Sunday in Ordinary Time

Year B/Lectionary no. 99

Mark 5:21-43

Narrator: When Jesus had crossed back to the other side of the Sea of Galilee in the boat, a large crowd gathered around him and he stayed close to the lake. One of the officials of the synagogue, a man named Jairus, came near. Seeing Jesus, he fell at his feet and made this earnest appeal:

Speaker: "My little daughter is critically ill. Please come and lay your hands on her so that she may get well and live."

Narrator: The two went off together and a large crowd followed, pushing against Jesus. There was a woman in the area who had been afflicted with a hemorrhage for a dozen years. She had received treatment at the hands of doctors of every sort and exhausted her savings in the process, yet she got no relief; on the contrary, she only grew worse. She had heard about Jesus and came up behind him in the crowd and put her hand to his cloak.

Speaker: "If I just touch his clothing, [" she thought, "] I shall get well."

Narrator: Immediately her flow of blood dried up and the feeling that she was cured of her affliction ran through her whole body. Jesus was immediately conscious that healing power had gone out from him. Wheeling about in the crowd, he began to ask,

Jesus: "Who touched my clothing?"

Narrator: His disciples said to him,

Speaker: "You can see how this crowd hems you in, yet you ask, 'Who touched me?' "

Narrator: Despite this, he kept looking around to see the woman who had done it. Fearful and beginning to tremble now as she realized what had happened, the woman came and fell in front of him and told him the whole truth. He said to her,

Jesus: "Daughter, it is your faith that has cured you. Go in peace and be free of this illness."

Narrator: He had not finished speaking when people from the official's house arrived saying,

Speaker: "Your daughter is dead. Why bother the Teacher further?"

Narrator: Jesus disregarded the report that had been brought and said to the official:

Jesus: "Fear is useless. What is needed is trust."

Narrator: He would not permit anyone to follow him except Peter, James, and James's brother John. As they approached the house of the synagogue leader, Jesus was struck by the noise of people wailing and crying loudly on all sides. He entered and said to them:

Jesus: "Why do you make this din with your wailing? The child is not dead. She is asleep."

Narrator: At this they began to ridicule him. Then he put them all out. Jesus took the child's father and mother and his own companions and entered the room where the child lay. Taking her hand he said to her,

Jesus: "Talitha, koum, ['' which means, ''] Little girl, get up."

Narrator: The girl, a child of twelve, stood up immediately and began to walk around. At this the family's astonishment was complete. He enjoined them strictly not to let anyone know about it, and told them to give her something to eat.

Speaker: This is the gospel of the Lord.

Fifteenth Sunday in Ordinary Time

Year B/Lectionary no. 105

Amos 7:12-15
Ephesians 1:3-14
Mark 6:7-13

AMOS Reading

Reader 1:   Amaziah (priest of Bethel) said to Amos,

Reader 2:   "Off with you, visionary, flee to the land of Judah! There earn your bread by prophesying, but never again prophesy in Bethel; for it is the king's sanctuary and a royal temple."

Reader 1:   Amos answered Amaziah,

Reader 3:   "I was no prophet, nor have I belonged to a company of prophets; I was a shepherd and a dresser of sycamores. The Lord took me from following the flock, and said to me, Go, prophesy to my people Israel."

Reader 1:   This is the Word of the Lord.

EPHESIANS Reading

Reader 1:   Praised be the God and Father of our Lord Jesus Christ, who has bestowed on us in Christ every spiritual blessing in the heavens!

Reader 2:   God chose us in him before the world began, to be holy and blameless in his sight, to be full of love;

Reader 3:   he likewise predestined us through Christ Jesus to be his adopted sons—such was his will and pleasure—that all might praise the divine favor he has bestowed on us in his beloved.

Reader 1:   It is in Christ and through his blood that we have been redeemed and our sins forgiven, so immeasurably generous is God's favor to us.

Reader 3:   God has given us the wisdom to understand fully the mystery, the plan he was pleased to decree in Christ, to be carried out in the fullness of time:

Reader 1:   namely, to bring all things in the heavens and on earth into one under Christ's headship.

Reader 2:   In him we were chosen;

Reader 3:   for in the decree of God, who administers everything according to his will and counsel, we were predestined to praise his glory by being the first to hope in Christ.

Reader 2:   In him you too were chosen;

Reader 1:   when you heard the glad tidings of salvation, the word of truth, and believed in it, you were sealed with the Holy Spirit who had been promised.

Reader 3:   He is the pledge of our inheritance, the first payment against the full redemption of a people God has made his own to praise his glory.

Reader 1:   This is the Word of the Lord.

MARK Reading

Reader 1:   Jesus summoned the Twelve and began to send them out two by two, giving them authority over unclean spirits. He instructed them to take nothing on the journey but a walking stick—no food, no traveling bag, not a coin in the purses in their belts. They were, however, to wear sandals.

Reader 2:   "Do not bring a second tunic," [he said, and added:] "Whatever house you find yourself in, stay there until you leave the locality. If any place will not receive you or hear you, shake its dust from your feet in testimony against them as you leave.''

Reader 3:   With that they went off, preaching the need of repentance. They expelled many demons, anointed the sick with oil, and worked many cures.

Reader 1:   This is the gospel of the Lord.

Sixteenth Sunday in Ordinary Time

Year A/Lectionary no. 107

Matthew 13:24-43

Speaker 1:   Jesus proposed to the crowd another parable:

Jesus: "The reign of God may be likened to a man who sowed good seed in his field. While everyone was asleep, his enemy came and sowed weeds through his wheat, and then made off. When the crop began to mature and yield grain, the weeds made their appearance as well. The owner's slaves came to him and said,

Speaker 1:   'Sir, did you not sow good seed in your field? Where are the weeds coming from?'

Jesus: "He answered,

Speaker 2:   'I see an enemy's hand in this.'

Jesus: "His slaves said to him,

Speaker 1:   'Do you want us to go out and pull them up?'

Speaker 2:   'No, [' he replied, '] pull up the weeds and you might take the wheat along with them. Let them grow together until harvest; then at harvest time I will order the harvesters, First collect the weeds and bundle them up to burn, then gather the wheat into my barn.' "

Speaker 1:   He proposed still another parable:

Jesus: "The reign of God is like a mustard seed which someone took and sowed in his field. It is the smallest seed of all, yet when full-grown it is the largest of plants. It becomes so big a shrub that the birds of the sky come and build their nests in its branches."

Speaker 1:	He offered them still another image:
Jesus:	"The reign of God is like yeast which a woman took and kneaded into three measures of flour. Eventually the whole mass of dough began to rise."
Speaker 1:	All these lessons Jesus taught the crowds in the form of parables. He spoke to them in parables only, to fulfill what had been said through the prophet:
Speaker 2:	"I will open my mouth in parables, I will announce what has lain hidden since the creation of the world."
Speaker 1:	Then, dismissing the crowds, he went home. His disciples came to him with the request,
Speaker 2:	"Explain to us the parable of the weeds in the field."
Speaker 1:	He said in answer:
Jesus:	"The farmer sowing good seed is the Son of Man; the field is the world, the good seed the citizens of the kingdom. The weeds are the followers of the evil one and the enemy who sowed them is the devil. The harvest is the end of the world, while the harvesters are the angels. Just as the weeds are collected and burned, so it will be at the end of the world. The Son of Man will dispatch his angels to collect from his kingdom all who draw others to apostasy, and all evildoers. The angels will hurl them into the fiery furnace where they will wail and grind their teeth. Then the saints will shine like the sun in their Father's kingdom. Let everyone heed what he hears!"
Speaker 2:	This is the gospel of the Lord.

Seventeenth Sunday in Ordinary Time

Year B/Lectionary no. 111

2 Kings 4:42-44
John 6:1-15

2 KINGS Reading

Narrator: A man came from Baal-shalishah bringing to Elisha, the man of God, twenty barley loaves made from the first-fruits and fresh grain in the ear.

Elisha: "Give it to the people to eat," [Elisha said.]

Narrator: But his servant objected,

Servant: "How can I set this before a hundred men?"

Elisha: "Give it to the people to eat, ['' Elisha insisted. ''] For thus says the Lord, 'They shall eat and there shall be some left over.' ''

Narrator: And when they had eaten, there was some left over, as the Lord had said.

This is the Word of the Lord.

JOHN Reading

Narrator: Jesus crossed the Sea of Galilee to the shore of Tiberias; a vast crowd kept following him because they saw the signs he was performing for the sick. Jesus then went up the mountain and sat down there with his disciples. The Jewish feast of Passover was near; when Jesus looked up and caught sight of a vast crowd coming toward him, he said to Philip,

Jesus: "Where shall we buy bread for these people to eat?"

Narrator:	(He knew well what he intended to do but he asked this to test Philip's response.) Philip replied,
Speaker:	"Not even with two hundred days' wages could we buy loaves enough to give each of them a mouthful!"
Narrator:	One of Jesus' disciples, Andrew, Simon Peter's brother, remarked to him,
Speaker:	"There is a lad here who has five barley loaves and a couple of dried fish, but what good is that for so many?"
Narrator:	Jesus said,
Jesus:	"Get the people to recline."
Narrator:	Even though the men numbered about five thousand, there was plenty of grass for them to find a place on the ground. Jesus then took the loaves of bread, gave thanks, and passed them around to those reclining there; he did the same with the dried fish, as much as they wanted. When they had had enough, he told his disciples,
Jesus:	"Gather up the crusts that are left over so that nothing will go to waste."
Narrator:	At this, they gathered twelve baskets full of pieces left over by those who had been fed with the five barley loaves. When the people saw the sign he had performed they began to say,
Speaker:	"This is undoubtedly the Prophet who is to come into the world."
Narrator:	At that, Jesus realized that they would come and carry him off to make him king, so he fled back to the mountain alone.
	This is the gospel of the Lord.

Seventeenth Sunday in Ordinary Time

Year C/Lectionary no. 112

Genesis 18:20-32

Narrator: The Lord said:

Lord: "The outcry against Sodom and Gomorrah is so great, and their sin so grave, that I must go down and see whether or not their actions fully correspond to the cry against them that comes to me. I mean to find out."

Narrator: While the two men walked on farther toward Sodom, the Lord remained standing before Abraham. Then Abraham drew nearer to him and said:

Abraham: "Will you sweep away the innocent with the guilty? Suppose there were fifty innocent people in the city; would you wipe out the place, rather than spare it for the sake of the fifty innocent people within it? Far be it from you to do such a thing, to make the innocent die with the guilty, so that the innocent and the guilty would be treated alike! Should not the judge of all the world act with justice?"

Narrator: The Lord replied,

Lord: "If I find fifty innocent people in the city of Sodom, I will spare the whole place for their sake."

Abraham: [Abraham spoke up again:] "See how I am presuming to speak to my Lord, though I am but dust and ashes! What if there are five less than fifty innocent people. Will you destroy the whole city because of those five?"

Lord: "I will not destroy it, [" he answered, "] if I find forty-five there."

Abraham: [But Abraham persisted, saying,] "What if only forty are found there?"

Lord:	[He replied,] "I will forbear doing it for the sake of the forty."
Abraham:	[Then he said,] "Let not my Lord grow impatient if I go on. What if only thirty are found there?"
Lord:	[He replied,] "I will forbear doing it if I can find but thirty there."
Narrator:	Still he went on,
Abraham:	"Since I have thus dared to speak to my Lord, what if there are no more than twenty?"
Lord:	"I will not destroy it, [" he answered, "] for the sake of the twenty."
Narrator:	But he still persisted:
Abraham:	"Please, let not my Lord grow angry if I speak up this last time. What if there are at least ten there?"
Lord:	"For the sake of those ten, [" he replied, "] I will not destroy it."
Narrator:	This is the Word of the Lord.

Eighteenth Sunday in Ordinary Time

Year B/Lectionary no. 114

Exodus 16:2-4,12-15
John 6:24-35

EXODUS Reading

Narrator: The whole Israelite community grumbled against Moses and Aaron. The Israelites said to them,

Speaker: "Would that we had died at the Lord's hand in the land of Egypt, as we sat by our fleshpots and ate our fill of bread! But you had to lead us into this desert to make the whole community die of famine!"

Narrator: Then the Lord said to Moses,

Lord: "I will now rain down bread from heaven for you. Each day the people are to go out and gather their daily portion; thus will I test them, to see whether they follow my instructions or not. I have heard the grumbling of the Israelites. Tell them: In the evening twilight you shall eat flesh, and in the morning you shall have your fill of bread, so that you may know that I, the Lord, am your God."

Narrator: In the evening quail came up and covered the camp. In the morning a dew lay all about the camp, and when the dew evaporated, there on the surface of the desert were fine flakes like hoarfrost on the ground. On seeing it, the Israelites asked one another, "What is this?" for they did not know what it was. But Moses told them,

Speaker: "This is the bread which the Lord has given you to eat."

Narrator: This is the Word of the Lord.

JOHN Reading

Narrator: When the crowd saw that neither Jesus nor his disciples were at the place where Jesus had eaten the bread, they too embarked in the boats and went to Capernaum looking for Jesus. When they found him on the other side of the lake, they said to him,

Speaker: "Rabbi, when did you come here?"

Narrator: Jesus answered them:

Jesus: "I assure you,
you are not looking for me because you have seen signs
but because you have eaten your fill of the loaves.
You should not be working for perishable food
but for food that remains unto life eternal,
food which the Son of Man will give you;
it is on him that God the Father has set his seal."

Speaker: [At this they said to him,] "What must we do to perform the works of God?"

Jesus: [Jesus replied:]

"This is the work of God:
have faith in the One he sent."

Speaker: "So that we can put faith in you, ['' they asked him, "] what sign are you going to perform for us to see? What is the 'work' you do? Our ancestors had manna to eat in the desert; according to Scripture, 'He gave them bread from the heavens to eat.' "

Jesus: [Jesus said to them:]

"I solemnly assure you,
it was not Moses who gave you bread from the heavens;
it is my Father who gives you the real heavenly bread.
God's bread comes down from heaven
and gives life to the world."

Speaker: "Sir, give us this bread always," [they besought him.]

Jesus: [Jesus explained to them:]

           "I myself am the bread of life.
           No one who comes to me shall ever be hungry,
           no one who believes in me shall thirst again."

Narrator: This is the gospel of the Lord.

Nineteenth Sunday in Ordinary Time

Year A/Lectionary no. 116

Matthew 14:22-33

Narrator:	After the crowds had their fill Jesus insisted that his disciples get into the boat and precede him to the other side. When he had sent them away, he went up on the mountain by himself to pray, remaining there alone as evening drew on.
Speaker:	Meanwhile the boat, already several hundred yards out from shore, was being tossed about in the waves raised by strong head winds.
Narrator:	At about three in the morning, he came walking toward them on the lake. When the disciples saw him walking on the water, they were terrified.
Speaker:	"It is a ghost!" [they said,]
Narrator:	and in their fear they began to cry out. Jesus hastened to reassure them:
Jesus:	"Get hold of yourselves! It is I. Do not be afraid!"
Narrator:	Peter spoke up and said,
Speaker:	"Lord, if it is really you, tell me to come to you across the water."
Jesus:	"Come!" [he said.]
Narrator:	So Peter got out of the boat and began to walk on the water, moving toward Jesus. But when he perceived how strong the wind was, becoming frightened he began to sink, and cried out,
Speaker:	"Lord, save me!"

Narrator:	Jesus at once stretched out his hand and caught him.
Jesus:	"How little faith you have! ["] he exclaimed. ["] Why did you falter?"
Narrator:	Once they had climbed into the boat, the wind died down. Those who were in the boat showed him reverence, declaring,
Speaker:	"Beyond doubt you are the Son of God!"
Narrator:	This is the gospel of the Lord.

Twenty-first Sunday in Ordinary Time

Year B/Lectionary no. 123

John 6:60-69

Narrator:	Many of the disciples of Jesus remarked,
Speaker:	"This sort of talk is hard to endure! How can anyone take it seriously?"
Narrator:	Jesus was fully aware that his disciples were murmuring in protest at what he had said.
Jesus:	"Does it shake your faith?" [he asked them.] "What, then, if you were to see the Son of Man ascend to where he was before. . . ? It is the spirit that gives life; the flesh is useless. The words I spoke to you are spirit and life. Yet among you there are some who do not believe."
Narrator:	(Jesus knew from the start, of course, the ones who refused to believe, and the one who would hand him over.) He went on to say:
Jesus:	"This is why I have told you that no one can come to me unless it is granted him by the Father."
Narrator:	From this time on, many of his disciples broke away and would not remain in his company any longer. Jesus then said to the Twelve,
Jesus:	"Do you want to leave me too?"
Narrator:	Simon Peter answered him,

Speaker: "Lord, to whom shall we go? You have the words of
            eternal life. We have come to believe; we are convinced that
            you are God's holy one."

Narrator: This is the gospel of the Lord.

Twenty-fourth Sunday in Ordinary Time

Year C/Lectionary no. 133

Luke 15:1-32

Narrator: The tax collectors and sinners were all gathering around to hear Jesus, at which the Pharisees and the scribes murmured,

Speaker: "This man welcomes sinners and eats with them."

Narrator: Then he addressed this parable to them:

Jesus: "Who among you, if he has a hundred sheep and loses one of them, does not leave the ninety-nine in the wasteland and follow the lost one until he finds it? And when he finds it, he puts it on his shoulders in jubilation. Once arrived home, he invites friends and neighbors in and says to them,

Speaker: 'Rejoice with me because I have found my lost sheep.'

Jesus: "I tell you, there will likewise be more joy in heaven over one repentant sinner than over ninety-nine righteous people who have no need to repent.

"What woman, if she has ten silver pieces and loses one, does not light a lamp and sweep the house in a diligent search until she has retrieved what she lost? And when she finds it, she calls in her friends and neighbors to say,

Speaker: 'Rejoice with me! I have found the silver piece I lost.'

Jesus: "I tell you, there will be the same kind of joy before the angels of God over one repentant sinner."

[Jesus said to them:] "A man had two sons. The younger of them said to his father,

Speaker: 'Father, give me the share of the estate that is coming to me.'

Jesus:	"So the father divided up the property. Some days later this younger son collected all his belongings and went off to a distant land, where he squandered his money on dissolute living. After he had spent everything, a great famine broke out in that country and he was in dire need. So he attached himself to one of the propertied class of the place, who sent him to his farm to take care of the pigs. He longed to fill his belly with the husks that were fodder for the pigs, but no one made a move to give him anything. Coming to his senses at last, he said:
Speaker:	'How many hired hands at my father's place have more than enough to eat, while here I am starving! I will break away and return to my father, and say to him, "Father, I have sinned against God and against you; I no longer deserve to be called your son. Treat me like one of your hired hands."'
Jesus:	"With that he set off for his father's house. While he was still a long way off, his father caught sight of him and was deeply moved. He ran out to meet him, threw his arms around his neck, and kissed him. The son said to him,
Speaker:	'Father, I have sinned against God and against you; I no longer deserve to be called your son.'
Jesus:	"The father said to his servants:
Narrator:	'Quick! bring out the finest robe and put it on him; put a ring on his finger and shoes on his feet. Take the fatted calf and kill it. Let us eat and celebrate because this son of mine was dead and has come back to life. He was lost and is found.'
Jesus:	"Then the celebration began.
	"Meanwhile the elder son was out on the land. As he neared the house on his way home, he heard the sound of music and dancing. He called one of the servants and asked him the reason for the dancing and the music. The servant answered,

Speaker: 'Your brother is home, and your father has killed the fatted calf because he has him back in good health.'

Jesus: "The son grew angry at this and would not go in; but his father came out and began to plead with him. He said in reply to his father:

Speaker: 'For years now I have slaved for you. I never disobeyed one of your orders, yet you never gave me so much as a kid goat to celebrate with my friends. Then, when this son of yours returns after having gone through your property with loose women, you kill the fatted calf for him.'

Narrator: 'My son, [' replied the father, '] you are with me always, and everything I have is yours. But we had to celebrate and rejoice! This brother of yours was dead, and has come back to life. He was lost and is found.' "

Speaker: This is the gospel of the Lord.

Twenty-fifth Sunday in Ordinary Time

Year A/Lectionary no. 134

Matthew 20:1-16

Reader 1:   Jesus told his disciples this parable: "The reign of God is like the case of the owner of an estate who went out at dawn to hire workmen for his vineyard. After reaching an agreement with them for the usual daily wage, he sent them out to his vineyard.

Reader 2:   "He came out about midmorning and saw other men standing around the marketplace without work, so he said to them,

Reader 3:   'You too go along to my vineyard and I will pay you whatever is fair.'

Reader 2:   "At that they went away. He came out again around noon and midafternoon and did the same. Finally, going out in late afternoon he found still others standing around. To these he said,

Reader 3:   'Why have you been standing here idle all day?'

Reader 1:   'No one has hired us,' [they told him.]

Reader 3:   [He said,] 'You go to the vineyard too.'

Reader 2:   "When evening came the owner of the vineyard said to his foreman,

Reader 3:   'Call the workmen and give them their pay, but begin with the last group and end with the first.'

Reader 1:   "When those hired late in the afternoon came up they received a full day's pay, and when the first group appeared they supposed they would get more; yet they received the same daily wage. Thereupon they complained to the owner,

Reader 2:   'This last group did only an hour's work, but you have put them on the same basis as us who have worked a full day in the scorching heat.'

Reader 3:   'My friend, [' he said to one in reply, '] I do you no injustice. You agreed on the usual wage, did you not? Take your pay and go home. I intend to give this man who was hired last the same pay as you. I am free to do as I please with my money, am I not? Or are you envious because I am generous?'

Reader 1:   "Thus the last shall be first and the first shall be last."

Reader 2:   This is the gospel of the Lord.

Twenty-sixth Sunday in Ordinary Time

Year C/Lectionary no. 139

Luke 16:19-31

Speaker: Jesus said to the Pharisees: "Once there was a rich man who dressed in purple and linen and feasted splendidly every day. At his gate lay a beggar named Lazarus who was covered with sores. Lazarus longed to eat the scraps that fell from the rich man's table. The dogs even came and licked his sores. Eventually the beggar died. He was carried by angels to the bosom of Abraham. The rich man likewise died and was buried. From the abode of the dead where he was in torment, he raised his eyes and saw Abraham afar off, and Lazarus resting in his bosom. He called out,

Rich Man: 'Father Abraham, have pity on me. Send Lazarus to dip the tip of his finger in water to refresh my tongue, for I am tortured in these flames.'

Abraham: 'My child, [' replied Abraham, '] remember that you were well off in your lifetime, while Lazarus was in misery. Now he has found consolation here, but you have found torment. And that is not all. Between you and us there is fixed a great abyss, so that those who might wish to cross from here to you cannot do so, nor can anyone cross from your side to us.'

Rich Man: 'Father, I ask you, then, [' the rich man said, '] send him to my father's house where I have five brothers. Let him be a warning to them so that they may not end in this place of torment.'

Abraham: [Abraham answered,] 'They have Moses and the prophets. Let them hear them.'

Rich Man: 'No, Father Abraham, [' replied the rich man. '] But if someone would only go to them from the dead, then they would repent.'

Abraham: [Abraham said to him,] 'If they do not listen to Moses and the prophets, they will not be convinced even if one should rise from the dead.' "

Speaker: This is the gospel of the Lord.

Twenty-seventh Sunday in Ordinary Time

Year B/Lectionary no. 141

Mark 10:2-16

Reader 1:   Some Pharisees came up and as a test began to ask Jesus whether it was permissible for a husband to divorce his wife. In reply he said,

Jesus: "What command did Moses give you?"

Reader 2:   [They answered,] "Moses permitted divorce and the writing of a decree of divorce."

Jesus: [But Jesus told them:] "He wrote that commandment for you because of your stubbornness. At the beginning of creation God made them male and female; for this reason a man shall leave his father and mother and the two shall become as one. They are no longer two but one flesh. Therefore let no man separate what God has joined."

Reader 1:   Back in the house again, the disciples began to question him about this. He told them,

Jesus: "Whoever divorces his wife and marries another commits adultery against her; and the woman who divorces her husband and marries another commits adultery."

Reader 2:   People were bringing their little children to him to have him touch them, but the disciples were scolding them for this. Jesus became indignant when he noticed it and said to them:

Jesus: "Let the children come to me and do not hinder them. It is to just such as these that the kingdom of God belongs. I assure you that whoever does not accept the kingdom of God like a little child shall not enter into it."

Reader 2:   Then he embraced them and blessed them, placing his hands on them.

Reader 1:   This is the gospel of the Lord.

Twenty-eighth Sunday in Ordinary Time

Year A/Lectionary no. 143

Matthew 22:1-14

Reader 1: Jesus began to address the chief priests and elders of the people, once more using parables.

Reader 2: "The reign of God may be likened to a king who gave a wedding banquet for his son. He dispatched his servants to summon the invited guests to the wedding, but they refused to come. A second time he sent other servants, saying:

Reader 3: 'Tell those who were invited, See, I have my dinner prepared! My bullocks and corn-fed cattle are killed; everything is ready. Come to the feast.'

Reader 2: "Some ignored the invitation and went their way, one to his farm, another to his business. The rest laid hold of his servants, insulted them, and killed them.

Reader 1: "At this the king grew furious and sent his army to destroy those murderers and burn their city. Then he said to his servants:

Reader 3: 'The banquet is ready, but those who were invited were unfit to come. That is why you must go out into the byroads and invite to the wedding anyone you come upon.'

Reader 1: "The servants then went out into the byroads and rounded up everyone they met, bad as well as good. This filled the wedding hall with banqueters.

Reader 2: "When the king came in to meet the guests, however, he caught sight of a man not properly dressed for a wedding feast.

Reader 3: 'My friend, [' he said, '] how is it you came in here not properly dressed?'

Reader 1:   "The man had nothing to say. The king then said to the attendants,

Reader 3:   'Bind him hand and foot and throw him out into the night to wail and grind his teeth.'

Reader 2:   "The invited are many, the elect are few."

Reader 1:   This is the gospel of the Lord.

Twenty-eighth Sunday in Ordinary Time

Year B/Lectionary no. 144

Mark 10:17-30

Narrator:	As Jesus was setting out on a journey a man came running up, knelt down before him and asked,
Speaker:	"Good Teacher, what must I do to share in everlasting life?"
Jesus:	[Jesus answered,] "Why do you call me good? No one is good but God alone. You know the commandments:

> 'You shall not kill;
> You shall not commit adultery;
> You shall not steal;
> You shall not bear false witness;
> You shall not defraud;
> Honor your father and your mother.' "

Speaker:	[He replied,] "Teacher, I have observed all these since my childhood."
Narrator:	Then Jesus looked at him with love and told him,
Jesus:	"There is one thing more you must do. Go and sell what you have and give to the poor; you will then have treasure in heaven. After that, come and follow me."
Narrator:	At these words the man's face fell. He went away sad, for he had many possessions. Jesus looked around and said to his disciples,
Jesus:	"How hard it is for the rich to enter the kingdom of God!"
Narrator:	The disciples could only marvel at his words. So Jesus repeated what he had said:

Jesus: "My sons, how hard it is to enter the kingdom of God! It is easier for a camel to pass through a needle's eye than for a rich man to enter the kingdom of God."

Narrator: They were completely overwhelmed at this, and exclaimed to one another,

Speaker: "Then who can be saved?"

Narrator: Jesus fixed his gaze on them and said,

Jesus: "For man it is impossible but not for God. With God all things are possible."

Narrator: Peter was moved to say to him:

Speaker: "We have put aside everything to follow you!"

Jesus: [Jesus answered:] "I give you my word, there is no one who has given up home, brothers or sisters, mother or father, children or property, for me and for the gospel who will not receive in this present age a hundred times as many homes, brothers and sisters, mothers, children and property—and persecution besides—and in the age to come, everlasting life."

Narrator: This is the gospel of the Lord.

Thirtieth Sunday in Ordinary Time

Year B/Lectionary no. 150

Jeremiah 31:7-9
Hebrews 5:1-6
Mark 10:46-52

JEREMIAH Reading

Reader 1:   Thus says the Lord:
Shout with joy for Jacob,
    exult at the head of nations;
    proclaim your praise and say:

Reader 2:   The Lord has delivered his people,
    the remnant of Israel.

Reader 3:   Behold, I will bring them back
    from the land of the north;
I will gather them from the ends of the world,
    with the blind and the lame in their midst,

Reader 2:   The mothers and those with child;
    they shall return as an immense throng.

Reader 1:   They departed in tears,
    but I will console them and guide them;

Reader 3:   I will lead them to brooks of water,
    on a level road, so that none shall stumble.

Reader 2:   For I am a father to Israel,
    Ephraim is my first-born.

HEBREWS Reading

Reader 1:   Every high priest is taken from among men and made their
representative before God, to offer gifts and sacrifices for
sins. He is able to deal patiently with erring sinners, for he

is himself beset by weakness and so must make sin offerings for himself as well as for the people. One does not take this honor on his own initiative, but only when called by God as Aaron was. Even Christ did not glorify himself with the office of high priest; he received it from the One who said to him,

Reader 2:   'You are my son;
                today I have begotten you'';

Reader 1:   just as he says in another place,

Reader 3:   ''You are a priest forever,
                according to the order of Melchizedek.''

MARK Reading

Narrator: As Jesus was leaving Jericho with his disciples and a sizable crowd, there was a blind beggar Bartimaeus (''son of Timaeus'') sitting by the roadside. On hearing that it was Jesus of Nazareth, he began to call out,

Bartimaeus: ''Jesus, son of David, have pity on me!''

Narrator: Many people were scolding him to make him keep quiet, but he shouted all the louder,

Bartimaeus: ''Son of David, have pity on me!''

Narrator: Then Jesus stopped and said,

Jesus: ''Call him over.''

Narrator: So they called the blind man over, telling him as they did so, ''You have nothing whatever to fear from him! Get up! He is calling you!'' He threw aside his cloak, jumped up and came to Jesus. Jesus asked him,

Jesus: ''What do you want me to do for you?''

Bartimaeus: ''Rabboni, ['' the blind man said, ''] I want to see.''

Jesus: [Jesus said in reply,] "Be on your way! Your faith has healed you."

Narrator: Immediately he received his sight and started to follow him up the road.

This is the gospel of the Lord.

Thirty-third Sunday in Ordinary Time

Year A/Lectionary no. 158

Matthew 25:14-30

Narrator: Jesus told this parable to his disciples:

Jesus: "A man was going on a journey. He called in his servants and handed his funds over to them according to each man's abilities. To one he disbursed five thousand silver pieces, to a second two thousand, and to a third a thousand. Then he went away. Immediately the man who received the five thousand went to invest it and made another five. In the same way, the man who received the two thousand doubled his figure. The man who received the thousand went off instead and dug a hole in the ground, where he buried his master's money. After a long absence, the master of those servants came home and settled accounts with them. The man who had received the five thousand came forward bringing the additional five.

Speaker: 'My lord, [' he said, '] you let me have five thousand. See, I have made five thousand more.'

Jesus: "His master said to him,

Narrator: 'Well done! You are an industrious and reliable servant. Since you were dependable in a small matter I will put you in charge of larger affairs. Come, share your master's joy!'

Jesus: "The man who had received the two thousand then stepped forward.

Speaker: 'My lord, [' he said, '] you entrusted me with two thousand and I have made two thousand more.'

Jesus: "His master said to him,

Narrator:	'Cleverly done! You too are an industrious and reliable servant. Since you were dependable in a small matter I will put you in charge of larger affairs. Come, share your master's joy!"
Jesus:	"Finally the man who had received the thousand stepped forward.
Speaker:	"My lord, [' he said, '] I knew you were a hard man. You reap where you did not sow and gather where you did not scatter, so out of fear I went off and buried your thousand silver pieces in the ground. Here is your money back.'
Narrator:	["His master exclaimed:] 'You worthless lazy lout! You know I reap where I did not sow and gather where I did not scatter. All the more reason to deposit my money with the bankers, so that on my return I could have had it back with interest. You, there! Take the thousand away from him and give it to the man with the ten thousand. Those who have will get more until they grow rich, while those who have not will lose even the little they have. Throw this worthless servant into the darkness outside, where he can wail and grind his teeth.' "
Speaker:	This is the gospel of the Lord.

Christic the King

Christ the King

Year A/Lectionary no. 161

Matthew 25:31-46

Narrator:	Jesus said to his disciples:
Jesus:	"When the Son of Man comes in his glory, escorted by all the angels of heaven, he will sit upon his royal throne, and all the nations will be assembled before him. Then he will separate them into two groups, as a shepherd separates sheep from goats. The sheep he will place on his right hand, the goats on his left. The king will say to those on his right:
Speaker:	'Come. You have my Father's blessing! Inherit the kingdom prepared for you from the creation of the world. For I was hungry and you gave me food. I was thirsty and you gave me drink. I was a stranger and you welcomed me, naked and you clothed me. I was ill and you comforted me, in prison and you came to visit me.'
Jesus:	"Then the just will ask him,
Narrator:	'Lord, when did we see you hungry and feed you or see you thirsty and give you drink? When did we welcome you away from home or clothe you in your nakedness? When did we visit you when you were ill or in prison?'
Jesus:	"The king will answer them:
Speaker:	'I assure you, as often as you did it for one of my least brothers, you did it for me.'
Jesus:	"Then he will say to those on his left:
Speaker:	'Out of my sight, you condemned, into that everlasting fire prepared for the devil and his angels! I was hungry and you gave me no food. I was thirsty and you gave me no drink. I

was away from home and you gave me no welcome, naked and you gave me no clothing. I was ill and in prison and you did not come to comfort me.'

Jesus: "Then they in turn will ask:

Narrator: 'Lord, when did we see you hungry or thirsty or away from home or naked or ill or in prison and not attend you in your needs?'

Jesus: "He will answer them:

Speaker: 'I assure you, as often as you neglected to do it to one of these least ones, you neglected to do it for me.'

Jesus: "These will go off to eternal punishment and the just to eternal life."

Narrator: This is the gospel of the Lord.